Ephesians:
A Jewish Perspective

A new translation that agrees with the rest of the Bible, printed with Messianic commentary and explanation of key theological issues addressed in Ephesians

By S. Kyle Moline

EPHESIANS: A Jewish Perspective

ISBN 978-1-4116-8602-1

Ephesians: a Messianic Understanding

Printed in United States of America

Cover art: the entrance to the library of Ephesus

All Bible quotations are translated by S. Kyle Moline.

Texts translated out of Greek were translated using the Nestlé–Aland, the Westcott–Hort, and the 1894 Scrivener Textus Receptus.

Texts translated out of Hebrew were translated using the Masoretic Text consulting both the Aleppo Codex and the Leningrad Codex.

Contents

Introduction to Ephesians

Before diving into the book of Ephesians, we need to know a few things. First, we need to know to whom he is writing. What was the political, cultural and theological background of the audience? Second, we need to know who the author is. By this, I do not mean just knowing his name; what we need to know is his personality and background, his culture and education. What linguistic differences exist between Shaul's native language, Hebrew, and the language that the letter is currently available in. "Was it written in Hebrew or Greek?" If in Hebrew, then we must be aware of the underlying Hebrew; if in Greek, we must be aware of the underlying Judaism. Once we know these things, we can see the internal evidence of the intent of the letter and the situation that it was addressing.

The earliest Greek texts of Ephesians are not actually addressed to the people of Ephesus. This makes a definitive interpretation based on the popular English translations dubious. However, the slim possibility that the change in the Greek texts was based on a history of the text which is no longer extant cannot be completely dismissed. Internal evidence does indicate that this letter was most probably Rabbi Shaul's final farewell before his execution, or at least that Rabbi Shaul thought that this was the case when he wrote it. There are passages that could have been specifically addressed to the people of Ephesus, but these would also be applicable to a number of other cities where idolatry was a major economic concern, such as Corinth, Rome, and Colossae. While it is doubtful that Ephesians was actually written solely to the congregations in Ephesus, Ephesus was reasonably typical of the cities in Asia Minor. While specifics of each city may change, certain commonalties hold true. Many people in this region made their living though idolatry. As a result of this uncertainty, we must be mindful of both possibilities as we interpret this book.

Many people view other books among Rabbi Shaul's writings as being more important than Ephesians due to the relative sizes of the books. However, since the majority of evidence indicates that this was written to the Messianic community at large, it is more universal. Being more universal, Ephesians is more authoritative if there are passages that seem to conflict with other writings of Rabbi Shaul. Some of Rabbi Shaul's other writings address local problems and situations, and therefore, the solutions that he proposes in some cases are not universally applicable. Some of the situations addressed in Ephesians are universally applicable, others are universally applicable to Gentiles within the Messianic community, while others are applicable to those suffering because they refuse to abandon their faith in HaShem.

The City of Ephesus

While the specifics of this city may not be universally relevant to the audience of Ephesians, the generalities were fairly common throughout Asia Minor in the outlying regions.

Ephesus was a port city in Western Asia Minor near the mouth of the Cayster River. The city was originally built near the site of a primitive temple to the Anatolian mother goddess. The area was already inhabited by Lelegians and Carians when the Ionian Greeks established the city of Ephesus.

The Greeks identified the Anatolian mother/fertility goddess with the Greek goddess Artemis. The worship of Artemis in this temple was influenced by the previous cult's worship practices and beliefs as the Greeks assimilated some of the worship practices of the native Anatolians. Even the idol of Artemis reflected the primitive Anatolian tendency toward paganism, having six breasts. This contrasted with the Greek idea of perfection being found in realism. These native Anatolians were most likely carrying on practices of the Hittites who had previously dominated the region.

Later, circa 560 BCE, a new temple, the Archaic Artimision was built. The Artimision was the primary temple to Artemis in the region. At this time, the city was moved from the northern slopes of Mt Pion to the plain south of the Archaic Artimision. This geography followed the traditional Greek style. Greek acropoli, the site for temples and ritually important buildings, were situated at the tops of hills and mountains while the actual cities where the people lived were at the bottoms of these hills.

When the first Archaic Artimision burned down, the new Artimision, was built. This classical structure was considered one of the Seven Wonders of the World during the Hellenistic period.

In 287 BCE, the city was moved to higher ground due to the danger of flooding. At this time the city was fortified and a new harbor and new streets were built.

As a result of the notoriety of the Artimision, silversmiths in the town made a great deal of money making and selling miniature replicas of the Artimision. These items were also used in worship of Artemis, presumably when the worshiper was unable to go to the temple. The silversmiths and their business allies opposed the monotheistic ideas of both Messianic Judaism and non-Messianic Judaism.

Rabbi Shaul

Ephesians was written by Rabbi Shaul (aka "Paul"). Who was this Rabbi? Most believers know that he wrote many of the Books (his letters) that are found in the Ketuvim Meshiachim (Messianic Scriptures, aka "the New Testament"). In Philippians Rabbi Shaul describes himself as "Circumcised the eighth day, of the Children of Israel, from the tribe of Binyamin, a Hebrew of Hebrews, according to the Torah a Parush (Pharisee)." In Acts 22:3 Rabbi Shaul is recorded as saying, "I am a Jew, born in Tarsus of Cilicia, raised in this city (Jerusalem) and trained at the feet of Gamli`el according to the exactness of the Torah of our fathers."

Being taught at the feet of Gamli`el is highly significant. First who is Gamli`el?

**Gamli`el I**, is also known as "Rabban Gamli'el the Elder." Gamli'el I was the grandson of Rabbi Hillel, the founder of Beyt Hillel (the more spiritual of the schools of Pharasaic theology). Gamli`el was in turn the leader of Beyt Hillel. He was the first person to hold the title "Rabban," which means "our teacher," or "our great one". This title is intended to convey the context "Rabbi of Rabbis." He is "the Elder" because he was the first of six Rabbinical leaders descended from Rabbi Hillel who were named "Gamli`el."

Gamli`el was a teacher of the Torah and Rosh Yishiva (head teacher at a Jewish seminary) of Beyt Hillel. Eventually, he became Nasi (leader) of the Sanhedrin. However this was after he taught Rabbi Shaul.

What is the significance of sitting at Gamli`el's feet? Only the best of the Rabbis went on to such a high level of education. This means that Rabbi Sha`ul had the First Century equivalent of a Doctorate in Rabbinical Studies and Rabbinical Literature. This explains his writing style. Rabbi Shaul uses Rabbinical literary techniques found in the Talmud. These techniques are from a different tradition than Western literary techniques; what is proper in the Western Tradition might be a mistake in the Talmudic Tradition, and vice-versa.

Beyt Hillel was the leading school of thought among the spiritual perspective of Pharisaic Judaism, as opposed to Beyt Shammai, the leading School of thought among the mechanical perspective of Pharisaic Judaism. Messiah frequently sided with Beyt Hillel in opposition to Beyt Shammai. This explains the continued attacks against His ministry by these legalists. Since Rabbi Shaul was educated in the spiritual understanding of Beyt Hillel it was almost instinctive for him to understand the spiritual nature of Messiah's explanation of the Torah.

This spiritual understanding did NOT mean a "theoretical" obedience by simply having faith. In fact, in Second Thessalonians 2:3 Rabbi Shaul describes the end time opposition to Messiah that people call "anti-Messiah" or "Anti-Christ" as "the man who separates himself from *Torah* " (2Thess 2:3) and as "Then the one who embodies separation from *Torah* " (2Thess 2:8). His description here reveals his opinion that disregard for the Torah is Satanic. It refers to the fact that Spiritualists see the Law as a gift from God that when followed leads us to improve our souls. The focus of Beyt Hillel's outlook on the Law was in how the law effects our souls and draws us closer to God. This is in opposition to Beyt Shammai's focus on our actions in accordance with the Law. The focus of Beyt Shammai's outlook on the Law was on our responsibility to perform actions in accordance with the Law.

Linguistically, Rabbi Shaul was fluent in Hebrew, and was an expert in Hebrew literature and Rabbinics. We know from the biblical account in Acts, Chapter 21, that he could speak some Greek, at least at a conversational level. We do not know for certain if he could read or write Greek. He may also have spoken some Aramaic. The possibility that he spoke some Aramaic is purely speculative since all the contemporary Jewish literature that has been recovered was written in Hebrew. Still, Aramaic was used by lawyers and politicians because there were so many legal contracts and international treaties and agreements written in Aramaic.

The Salutations of Rabbi Shaul's Letters

The addressing on many of the letters that Rabbi Shaul wrote is to the word "ekklesia," which is discussed in detail in "Translational Notes." Other letters were addressed to the "αγιοις / αγιων (hagios)" which means "Holy Ones" or "Purified Ones."

Of Rabbi Shaul's letters, those addressed to the community at large are frequently easier to understand. He is trying to write to the common man. Rabbi Kefa states, in Second Kefa 3:15&16, that Rabbi Shaul frequently goes over the heads of his audience and can therefore be misunderstood. So, even those letters addressed to the hagios contain rabbinical elements that may need explanation for the benefit of most readers today.

Ephesians being addressed to the hagios fits the context in that Rabbi Shaul was saying "good bye" to the Messianic Community at large. He is giving a final, personal message to all the people in the congregations that he played an important role in starting.

The fact that Ephesians was not actually addressed to the Ephesians in the oldest texts is very important also. Since it was addressed to the Messianic community as a whole, especially those congregations in Asia Minor, it is more universal than letters written to a specific congregation or city.

Translational Notes

General Notes:
Interpretation is an inherant part of translation. A translator may attempt to translate a body of text literally, but even reading the text is a process of interpretation. Even reading one's native language or listening to somone else speaking is a process of interpreting. So, any translation carries some of the translator's beliefs within the text. In Judaism there are rules for interpretation which are applied to Scripture. Rabbi Shaul was well aware of these rules. In fact in various places in his letters Rabbi Shaul intentionally includes wording that imploys these rules in his reading of the Tanakh. If these rules are applied to the text, our translation cannot go far from his original intention. When we also consider biographical facts about the author, our options in interpretation are further narrowed. Historical research concerning the intended audience and the world at large at the time improves our accuracy even more.

The basic concepts of Scriptural interpretation include:

1: If we accept that the entire body of Scripture is true, then no verse can contradict any other verse.

2: The Seven Rules of Hillel and the Thirteen Rules of Ismael for interpreting Scripture are not simply applied to Scripture after the fact, they are part of the composition of Scripture.

3: Since science is the search for the truths of the physical world and the Bible is entirely true, there is no disagreement betweem proven scientific facts and the actual meaning of the Scriptures.

4: There are three distinct levels of Divine inspiration found in the Tanakh, and these three levels are found in the Messianic Scriptures as well.

   a: As a result of this, the writings of Rabbi Shaul must be interpreted so that they argee with everything that Yshu`a said, as recorded in the Bsorat.

   b: Everything that Yshu`a said as recorded in the Bsorat, must be interpreted to agree with the Torah which was dictated letter by letter and which is defined in John 1:1-5 as being Messiah.

5: Many Hebrew and Greek words change their definitions based on context. The context with which we are working is the entire Bible.

6: The juxtaposition of passages is indicative of interrelation between passages. Because God is logical, there is a logical progression from one thought to the next in the Bible. Therefore, each passage follows the previous passage for a logical reason. These reasons cannot be overlooked when interpreting or translating a passage.

7: Since Greek was effectively a "dead language" prior to the translations of the Greek manuscripts into English, many of the definitions in our current lexicons are actually probable definitions. The supposed probability of some of these is based purely on Catholic tradition and not on an independent source or a biblical source.

8: There is a cultural context to all writings. The text must be read within the cultural and religious context of

First Century Judaism taking into account the author's conviction that Yshu`a is the Messiah.

There is a tendancy for many people to assume that the oldest English translations are more correct. The King James Translation has many supporters who feel that newer translations represent change. This idea is actually quite false. Since the time of the writing of the The King James Translation, over eight humdered words, which are each used multiple times in the KJV, have had their definitions changed by the ongoing development of the English language. Also, mankind has progressed in the science of archeology and can more accurately date ancient manuscripts than was previously possible. Furthermore, prior to the advent of the Modern Messianic Movement, Christians did not have access to source materaial describing the doctrinal issues that were being debated amoung First Century CE Jewish theologians. Today more than ever, we have the ability to accurately translate the Messianic Scriptures so that they convey their intended message

Notes on the Original Language:
In this particular case we must also be mindful that it is highly unlikely that Ephesians was originally written in Greek. We know that Rabbi Shaul was fluent in speaking, reading and writing Hebrew, and that he was an expert in Hebrew literature. We also know that he spoke some Greek, and probably spoke it fairly well. We have no idea if Rabbi Shaul could write Greek at all. There are several different ancient Greek versions of this book. This seems unlikely if the book were written in Greek. If Rabbi Shaul wrote in Greek we would expect all the manuscripts be the same.

There are also practical reasons why Rabbi Shaul would not have written his letters in Greek. While the various cities to which he wrote letters had populations that spoke Hebrew, Greek, Latin, or Aramaic as their primary language, all the congregational leaders spoke, read and wrote Hebrew. Rabbi Shaul quite probably also wrote Hebrews. Since the congregations in Galilee would not speak Greek at all it would not have made sense for Rabbi Shaul to write to these congregations in Greek.

There is another factor that comes into play when we investigate the entire library of the Greek manuscripts. When we look at the many different Greek texts, we must ask why there are different versions of the Greek texts. If Rabbi Shaul wrote in Greek wouldn't all the manuscripts be the same?

There is also internal evidence to suggest that Hebrew may have been the original language of many of his letters. The use of the word "νομος (nomos)" can be perplexing in Rabbi Sha`ul's writing. He seems to change his stance on this "nomos" repeatedly. There is no wording used in the Greek to differentiate between the "nomos" he loves, and the "nomos" he hates. If the Rabbi had been writing in Greek he would have used terms that differentiated between these types of "nomos." This indicates a Hebrew original text.

The Greek "nomos" can be used to translate at least 14 words and phrases from a Hebrew text:

1. Torah – Instruction: Multiple meanings depending on context. It always includes the Torah Shebi Khetav, but can also include the rest of the Tanakh and the Torah Shebe al Peh depending on the context of the writing.

2. Torah Shebi Khetav – The Written Torah: The Torah that God gave to Mosheh: B'reshit (Genesis), Sh'mot (Exodus), Vayikra (Leviticus), B'midbar (Numbers), Dvarim (Deuteronomy). Also called "Torah."

3. Tanakh (TNK from Torah, Naviyim, and Ketuvim (the Instruction, Prophets, and Holy Writings) - also called the "Old Testament."

4. Torah Shebe al Peh – Oral Torah: The instructions that HaShem gave to Mosheh on Mt Sinai and Mosheh transmitted orally to Yehoshua and Aharon.

5. Mitzvah (Pl: Mitzvot) – Commandment(s): All 613 Commandments in the Torah.

6. Mishpat (Pl: Mishpatim) – Law(s): The Laws among the 613 that are so obvious that even an Atheist accepts them as required for society to function. Example: "Don't Murder."

7. `Ed (Pl: `Edot) – Remembrances: The Laws among the 613 that are designed to strengthen our faith. Example: The Commandment to observe Passover

8. Chuk (Pl: Chukim) – Decrees: The Laws from among the 613 that HaShem never explains. Example: the dietary prohibitions.

9. Halakhah – The Walk/The Way: The application of the Torah, both Written and Oral, to our lives. This was based on the Oral Torah.

10. Mishpatim Sofrim - the Rulings/Laws of the Sofrim (Scribes): these rulings, originally intended to help people obey the Mitzvot by separating them from temptation, eventually became so complicated that they conflicted with themselves.

11. Neder (Pl: Nedarim) – Vow(s): Personal oaths that do NOT conflict with the Torah and are taken as a personal addition to Torah. The Torah Shebi Khetav states that these vows are as binding as they would be if they were written in the Torah Shebi Khetav itself. The purpose of such oaths is to strengthen one's ability to serve HaShem. Example: an alcoholic may take a neder prohibiting him from even entering a bar. This would help him avoid the temptation to get drunk.

12. Chumrah (pl: Chumrot) – Severity/Restriction: Rabbinical ordinances designed to keep the people from violating the Torah. These may be addressed to particular regions or circumstances. Example: Rabbi Sha`ul forbid Messianic Jews in Corinth and Rome from pretending to be homosexual. In Rome and Corinth it was socially unacceptable for a man to be openly heterosexual. Many Greek heterosexuals pretended to be homosexual to fit into society. Because it is encouraging evil to pretend that sin is socially acceptable, Rabbi Sha`ul made this Chumrah.

13. Civil Law: the laws of the country that we live in.

14. Legalism: (1) a perversion of the Law that misuses the Commandments as a way to earn salvation. (2) a dedication to the Code of Law above all else. This

form of legalism is actually idolatrous since it sets up the Law as an idol to be worshiped, since the legalist looses sight of the goal of the Torah: to bring us closer to HaShem.

15. Legalism: (1) a perversion of the Law that misuses the Commandments as a way to earn salvation. (2) a dedication to the Code of Law above all else. Legalism is actually idolatrous since it sets up the Law as an idol to be worshiped. There was no Hebrew word for legalism in Rabbi Shaul's time; so, Rabbi Shaul would have to make up a word or phrase. Based on the terminology for "paganism" in Hebrew ("eliliyot" or "avodat elilim"), he would most likely have used "Mishpatot," which would have been mistranslated as "nomos (law)" in Greek or "Avodat Mishpatim," which would have been mistranslated "ergon nomos" (works of the Law)."

With this understanding, we see that we must use the context to determine which "nomos" the rabbi means in each instance. Obviously he agrees with Yshu`a's stance that the both the Written and Oral Torah are good, but that many of the man-made laws are not good. While "Chumrah," "Torah," and "Mitzvot" all translate into Greek as "Nomos," They have three different meanings. Yshu`a supported the eternal validity of the Torah and the Mitzvot in Matthew 5:17-19, but frequently opposed certain Chumrot because they conflicted with the Spirit of God's Law. We would expect an Apostle of Yshu`a to hold the same opinion. When the reader is versed in the Torah and reads the various books "cover to cover," Rabbi Shaul does display that he holds this opinion. However, the reader becomes aware that the translation that we have today lacks clarifying words when "law" is mentioned. This situation can be overcome though a holistic approach to the Bible as one continuous body of Scripture.

Notes on the Word Ekklesia:
Of particular interest in translating Rabbi Shaul's writings, is the word "εκκλησια (ekklesia)." For centuries Believers have accepted the Catholic Church's tradition for defining the word. This tradition is to use the word "Church," and to presume that this refers to the Catholic Church. With the majority of the world's Christian denominations believing that the Catholic Church is not the body of believers founded by the Messiah, one would expect this word to be examined more thoroughly.

Linguistically, we know that the Teutonic language from which English evolved contained the word from which "church" was derived. The word "ᛣᚱᛁᛇ (krich)" meant "a circle of trees used for human sacrifice." While the language has developed over the centuries, and the definition has shifted along with the culture, this word still seems to be an unsatisfactory translation.

Knowing that Rabbi Shaul almost certainly wrote in Hebrew, we should look at the Hebrew words that He might have used that aproximate what we know of the word "ekklesia." Some Hebrew words that are likely are: "קְהִלָּה (k'hilah – assembly, congregation or community)," "קְהִלּוֹת (k'hilot – assemblies, congregations, or communities)," "קְהִלָּת (k'hilat – assemblies, congregations or communities)," "קֹהֶלֶת (kohelet – assembly of leaders, counselors)," The Septuagint uses "sungogen (synagogue)" to translate various forms of "k'hilah." In the Septugint, we also find "Kohelet" translated as "Εκκλησιαστου (Ekklesiastou)" "Εκκλησιαστης

(Ekklesiastes).” In this case it is a nickname for King Solomon used because he surrounded himself with leaders in everey field, so that he always had expert advise no matter what the subject in question. This shows that the older and more established meaning for “εκκλησια (ekklesia)" referenced the leaders as opposed to the body as a whole.

It has been generally assumed that “ekklesia” means “called out ones.” It is the specific application that comes into question. In modern English, we distinguish between those with a “job,” those with a “career,” those with a “profession,” and those with a “calling.” It is not too far-fetched to investigate the same usage here especially with the variant meanings derived from the same Hebrew root.

Knowing that, in Hebrew, words often have multiple definitions from which we select the definition that makes the most sense, one must wonder is this could be true in Greek as well. A quick look through a Greek-English lexicon shows that this is in fact the case. So, a word analysis is in order. There were four variants of “ekklisia” used in the translations of Shaul’s writings. When looking all of these up, we find that some could only be translated with “[Messianic] Rabbinate” to make sense, and others could only be translated with “[Messianic] Community.” Interestingly, there was a significant distribution of these based on the spelling of the Greek word.

Verses that could only be translated as “[Messianic] Rabbinate” always used “εκκλησια (ekklesia)" or “εκκλησιας (ekklesias)." Verses that could only be translated as “[Messianic] Community” always used “εκκλησιαν (ekklesian)" or “εκκλησιαι (ekklesiai)." There were some that could go either way in three of the spellings, but "εκκλησιαν (ekklesian)" seems to almost always be used to refer to the entire community or synagogue.

We must also take into account practical matters when examining the question of the translation of the word "ekklesia" and its derivatives. When we consider the wisdom of the letters, it would also be unwise to write a letter to a group of people that you do not know exceedingly well when you do not have the opportunity to explain any points that may be unclear. Many of the topics that Shaul dicusses are of vital importance, but at times he can get theoretical. While it is easy for a fellow rabbi to comprehend his points, a person who had just stoped worshiping statues last week would find parts of his letters baffling. This leads one to believe that they were addressed to the Messianic Rabbis leading the Messianic congregations of the area.

When we consider the ethics of the letters, writing them to the local Rabbinical community would be more ethical. Writing to the congregants directly could be seen as undermining the authority of the local rabbis. Since Rabbi Sha`ul is recorded behaving in a way that supported the established Messianic Jewish Community and the leadership of the Messianic Beyt Din, it is highly unlikely that he would violate his own demonstrated ethics. The Rabbi's own ethics demontrate that is is highly probable that he was addressing the Spiritual Leaders of the communities.

Stylisticly, Rabbi Sha`ul uses literary styles that would be above the heads of most people, and are from a culture that is foreign to the congregants in the regions outside Israel. In his Letters Rabbi Sha`ul assumes that the reader is an expert in Judaism. For exmple: in I Corinthians, Chapter 10, Rabbi Sha`ul assumes that the reader is versed with the Rabbinical definition of "Lo tirtzach (Don't murder)" , the rabbinical princle of Pikuach Nefesh (the principle that some Commandments [never those prohibiting murder, idolatry, or sexual immorality] may be set aside in order to save a human life), and the "Kal V'homer" (light to heavy) rule of interpreting Scripture. This provides a strong indication that this letter was addressed to the Messianic Rabbis of Corinth. The salutation of the letter is to the "ekklesiai."

Based on the majority of evidence, the letters addressed to the "ekklasiai" seem to have been addressed to the rabbis of the congregations in the various communities, while letters addressed to the "hagios" were addressed to the congregation at large. The local rabbis would be fully equipt to act upon the letter in a way that best communicated the intentions of Rabbi Sha`ul. Whether they translated and explained the Hebrew or taught the message in their own words or established policies to attain the goals of the letters would depend on which measures would best glorify the Ruach HaKodesh (the Holy Spirit), and bring people into a stable relationship with Messiah.

Notes on Names:
Since it is not proper to translate or change names, the names in this translation and the notes are left in their original form.

Elohim = God (denotes the enire unity of God)
Yshu`a [HaMashiach]= the Messiah
Rabbi Shaul = Paul
Rabbi Kefa = Peter

EPHESIANS

with commentary

EPHESIANS

1 [1] *[From:] Sha'ul, by Elohim's decree, a representative* of the Messiah Yshuà*
To: Sanctified People being on _______ [in Ephesus], and having moral conviction in, the Messiah, Yshuà,* [2] *Chesed to*

---

* 1:1a — In today's culture, believers have changed the meaning of the Greek word "αποστολος(apostolos)." People use the word "apostle" as if this title was both greater than the reality of it and also more inaccessible. The Greek word simply means that the person represents [Yshu`a and thus God] in his actions and seeks to advance [God's kingdom]. Today people think that they cannot reach this level of service to God, so they settle for less holiness in their lives than they could achieve if they knew that it was possible to go beyond these man-made restrictions.

* 1:1b — This salutation indicates that Rabbi Shaul was addressing this letter to the entire congregation. The older, more reliable manuscripts do not contain the words "in Ephesus." Origen did not have the city name here and Marcion claimed that it was written to the Laodicians. Also, there are no references to particular individuals. Thus, it is very possible that it was not specifically written to the Congregations in Ephesus. In fact, it may have been written much like a form letter with the carrier inserting the name of the city in which he was reading it at the time. When the complete body of Greek texts are examined, there

is little evidence to support the idea that this letter was specific to the Ephesians. However there is little doubt that Ephesus was one of the cities where this letter would be read.

The Greek uses "αγιοις (hagios)" which means "Holy Ones" or "Purified Ones." From this we know that this letter was addressed to the general populace of the various congregations. We do not see as much use of complicated rabbinics as we see in Shaul's letters addressed to the "εκκλησιαι (ekklesiai)," the Rabbinates of various cities.

Origen – a.k.a "Origen of Alexandria," 185-254 CE. Origen was a philosopher who lived during the era when believers in Messiah were assimilating many pagan ideas. He was a believer in Messiah who defended the belief against attacks from pagan philosophers using their own philosophy. He invented the Doctrine of the "Trinity" (based upon the Middle Platonic triadic emanation schemas), and several other extra-biblical and anti-biblical theologies. He greatly influenced how much pagan philosophy the early Catholic church would first assimilate when it was founded in 325 CE. While Origen is considered by many to be a "church father," his most long lasting influence was to bring pagan philosophy into the Gentile expression of belief in Yshu`a.

Marcion – c.84-160 CE. Marcion was the son of the bishop of Sinope. Marcion established his own sect in 144 CE based on his idea that the God of the Tanakh was different and inferior to the God of the Messianic Scriptures. He was excommunicated for this heresy.

you and peace from Elohim, our Father and the Adonai
Yshuà, the Messiah. *
[3] *Praised be Elohim, Father of Adoneynu* * *Yshuà, the*
Messiah, who has blessed us with every spiritual blessing in

---

* 1:2 — The Greek word used here does not translate to a single English word and the Hebrew word for the Jewish theological concept does not entirely match the Greek word popularly used to translate it. The Hebrew word "chesed" means "acts of kindness motivated only by love." The Greek word used "χαρις (karis)" means "gracious in manner and action especially as the result of divine influence." This word is usually translated with the English word "grace" to which Christianity has appended additional meaning to make the translation work in a rough manner that varies from denomination to denomination. The variation in the understanding of the English word leads us to go back to the Hebrew so that we have a complete and accurate understanding of the verse.

Chesed is the motivating force behind God's decision to save our souls when we accept Yshu`a as Messiah and dedicate ourselves to following Him. It is also the motivation that leads saved people to obey God's Commandments without asking for rewards for our actions. So, in one word Rabbi Shaul expresses his desire for the souls of the people to be and remain saved as well as wishing that they obey God's Law of their own choice out of love for God.

Additionally, wishing Chesed upon a saved person indicates Rabbi Shaul's belief that a person can reject their salvation and become damned. He discusses this more obviously in Hebrews 10:26-29.

* 1:3a — The use of "kurios (Lord)" here looses meaning in translation from Rabbi Shaul's native Hebrew into Greek and then into English. "Kurios" is used in Greek to translate the Hebrew word "Adonai," as is the English "the Lord." This Hebrew word is not simply a title, it is one of the two euphemisms used for the Tetragrammaton, the four-letter name of God. As such, it is a proper noun referring to God the Father. From the rabbi's point of view, this is a reference to the divinity of Yshu`a HaMashiach.

* 1:3b — The Greek word "ευλογησας (eulogesas)" translated here as "blessed" as well as the Greek word "ευλογια (eulogia)" translated here as "blessing" both refer to good things being said. This indicates a Jewish concept that goes back to Genesis, chapter one and is carried forward. God's words have power and it is through His words that all things are accomplished.

If one looks at this verse using the Sod level of interpretation, it is easy to see the connection between this word choice and John 1:1-5 where Yshu`a is called "the Word" and states that, "All things came to be through Him, and without Him nothing made had being," John 1:3.

Sod level of Interpretation – This level of interpretation looks at the poetics of word choice. See Appendix Five for a more complete definition.

Heaven through Messiah. * [4] *Just as He chose us before the*

---

* 1:3c — The term "every spiritual blessing in Heaven" indicates that there is more than one blessing being spoken of in this passage. Salvation is the first thing to come into most people's minds, and of course this in one of the blessings to which this term refers. The others are the Commandments themselves.

Deuteronomy 11:26&27 says, "Behold: I set before you today a blessing and a curse. The blessing: that you listen to the Commandments of Adonai, your God that I command you today." This tells us that obeying God is a blessing thus all the commandments are potential blessings. The Commandments are designed to bring us closer to God in this life, while Messiah's death on our behalf brings us closer to God in the next life. Obedience to the Torah prepares us to accept Yshu`a as Messiah, and the gratitude we feel once we accept Him as Messiah inspires us to be more obedient to God, which in turn blesses us with a greater understanding of Messiah, which makes us even more grateful for what he did on our behalf, and further inspires us. This cycle draws us closer and closer to God.

* 1:4-6 — HaShem chose to create mankind to fellowship with Him. He created Adam and Eve perfect. Sadly, Adam and Eve chose to mar that perfection. HaShem knew that mankind would rebel against Him, but loved us anyway and created a means of restoration through Messiah. In this way mankind may see the error of sin and seek restoration through Messiah. This passage has frequently been

misunderstood to indicate some sort of predestination.

Rabbi Shaul, while supporting the sovereignty of HaShem, never renounced the individual's role in choosing to accept Yshu`a as Messiah or in choosing between righteousness and sin. In light of these other writings, we cannot claim that Rabbi Shaul would change his position in these verses.

Additionally, the wording here is analogous to wording in several Jewish prayers. It is well known that though HaShem chose Israel for a particular purpose, we have not all worked for that purpose, and at times the majority of Israel did not work towards the purpose for which we were chosen, but the choosing is still valid and we have a responsibility to work towards the goal that we were chosen to accomplish.

Finally, Messiah Himself made it clear that He did not want anyone to be damned. While Messiah has provided for the Salvation of all Mankind, some people reject Him and the salvation that he provides. Rabbi Shaul would not defy Yshu`a's teachings by opposing the hope of the Gospel and setting up a tyranny of predestination.

The issue of predestination has arisen in both Jewish and Christian thought. While Christianity is split on the issue, Judaism has rejected it based on the fact that predestination would require God to commit evil actions. Specifically, the Jewish understanding which Rabbis Shaul used in First Corinthians, chapter ten, of the Hebrew "Lo tirtzach (Don't murder) is that ending the life of a person out of

creation of the universe to exist holy and sinless before Him in love. * *[5] He established before the beginning that by the actions of Yshuà the Messiah we would be adopted as His sons** *— according to the satisfaction of His desire — [6] So to*

---

hatred is a sin and thus the even more significant act of preventing a person's salvation is even more sinful. While there are valid reason's to end another person's physical life (self defense, defense of others, execution of criminals for certain crime as laid out in the Bible), there is no valid reason to cause or even permit another person's damnation. Since God never commits any evil action, predestination must be a myth.

Rabbi Akiva summed up the reality of the situation in a single sentence "Everything is known and freewill is given." In other words, while God knows that some people will make evil choices, He does not impose that evil upon them.

* 1:4 — God created this world for mankind to fellowship with Him in the World. As such the world was created on a foundation of Torah observance. God did NOT create a flawed world and then have to give us instructions work around His mistakes. He created the world perfect with a specific purpose. As such, sinful actions have physical, emotional and spiritual repercussions even without God punishing us for our misdeeds. Using the world as a venue for evil is a misuse of the world and causes the world harm. Using our bodies as a tool of evil is a misuse of out bodies and causes us harm.

* 1:5 — This verse is especially difficult to translate because the Greek words used are used in the context of the Bible which is unusual for Greek. The Greek word "προορισας (proorisas)" usually means "to establish boundaries or limitations of techniques prior to beginning work on the project or task in question." In the biblical sense it refers to those things that God created or ordained prior to creating the world.

Since God only created the world so that humanity could live on the earth and fellowship with Him, the world was created in a way that is potentially beneficial to humans who live without sin. Because God knew that mankind would fall into sin before he began creation, He established the means of our salvation before allowing us the opportunity to fail morally.

God did NOT create evil. He defined "good" and those things that are outside of the boundaries that He established for defining "good" are by their lack of goodness, evil.

"Sons of God" here denotes a loving Father-child relationship. This relationship contains the hierarchical, and authoritative principles of a traditional Jewish father and son relationship. In certain passages of the Tanakh, the Israelites are referred to as "sons of God." This same relationship applies. It should also be noted that this also hints at the idea of non-Jews being grafted into the Jewish community since he uses one of the most complimentary terms of the Jewish people and uses it to refer to both Jews and non-Jews who follow Yshu`a.

*the praise of the manifest glory of His chesed**, *with which He favored us in love.*

[7] *In whom, we have redemption because of His blood — the pardon of mistakes by means of the abundance of His chesed,* * [8] *which abounds for us in all wisdom and intelligence.* * [9] *He has revealed to us the secret of what He desires according to His kindness which He exhibited in*

---

* 1:6 — The manifest glory of God refers to the example set by Yshu`a. In the secular sense "glory" simply means something that makes someone or something praiseworthy. When referring to God, there are two factors to consider. First, that God is not hypocritical, which is to say that He obeys the Commandments that He gave to us. Second, that despite being in a position to justly punish humanity for our sins both personal and collective, He chose to suffer and take our punishment on Himself. Yshu`a embodies both of these in a way that allowed for us to see Him demonstrate God's Glory.

In the various Pagan religions, the mythological "gods" were corrupted by their own power. Even those that were considered "good" by their worshipers were recorded in Pagan myths as having committed actions that the Bible condemns as evil.

Prior to the coming of Yshu`a, the fact that Adonai obeys all of His Mitzvot was certainly a belief of Judaism. However the observance of many of His Mitzvot was metaphorical due to the fact that God, in His totality, is not a physical being. A Pagan could also say that Adonai, as a non-physical entity did not have to overcome temptation. Once Yshu`a came, no such arguments could be made with any credibility.

* 1:7 — The words "redemption" and "pardon" express two different thoughts that are related. A "pardon" is a reprieve from punishment. The pardoned person is still guilty. Redemption is the removal of the person from evil, and bringing him back to God. Therefore "pardon" refers to our Salvation, and "redemption" refers to the righteousness taught by Messiah.

Yshu`a came to save humanity from sin, not just from punishment. He does forgive sins and thus we are spared punishment, but that is not all. Sin, in and of itself, is destructive; it destroys the body, mind, and soul. Messiah came to save us from the bondage of committing sins as well as from the punishment deserved by sinners.

* 1:8 — As mentioned above, this world was created based upon God's Laws. The world was designed as a venue for obeying God's Commandments. Thus when we put God's creation to purposes for which it was not designed, destruction results. Therefore a wise person sees God's Commandments as a blessing. They are instructions for how to live a happy life. An intelligent person observes how God's laws work within the physical, chemical, and biological Laws and understands that God's Law is in harmony with the real world.

Mitzvot – the 613 Commandments in the Torah

Chesed – acts of kindness motivated only by love

Himself. * [10] *for the stewardship of the fullness of the proper time — to bring together as one everything, in Messiah – the things in Heaven and the things on earth.* *

---

* 1:9 — Verse 7 could lead one to see Messiah alone as the source of salvation as if He was separate from God. In this verse, that misconception is dismissed. God saw within Himself a goodness and compassion that are the reason that He established salvation through Messiah's atoning blood. Some people see God the Father who gives us the Law as an opposition to Messiah. This was never the case. Both the Law and Messiah's self-sacrifice are designed to draw us closer to God.

Additionally, Psalm 22:17 (22:16 in Christian Bibles), which describes Messiah's execution reads "…Like a lion My hands and feet." This passage seems incomprehensible to someone who has not studied Talumd Bavli, Tractate Sukkah, 52a. This discussion in the Talmud says that Messiah Ben David (King Messiah) would come after Messiah Ben Yosef (Suffering Servant Messiah). Now, we draw upon other facts to complete our understanding. King David was from the Tribe of Judah. The tribal banner of Judah was a lion. Judah, the tribal patriarch, did not rise to the role of leader until he offered himself in place of his brother, Benjamin. From the Bsorat, we know that the two manifestations of Messiah are manifestations of the same Messiah coming and then returning. When we combine all these facts, we see that Messiah, when He died for our sins, became Messiah Ben David by means of the wounds in His hands and feet. Thus

Yshu`a changed roles being now prepared for the accomplishment of those messianic prophecies concerning His return. Which leads into the next verse…

* 1:10 — This verse does not mean that HaShem will become subordinate to Messiah. The Greek word "οικονομιαν (oikonomian)" means "stewardship." A steward is a person who takes care of something for its owner. In this case, Yshu`a brings together Heaven and earth and rules while God is still King of the Universe. The intricacies of the interrelation of Father, Son, and Spirit are beyond human understanding.

Yshu`a said that the father who sent Him was greater than Him, and that he and the Father are one. How this can be can only be understood after we enter Heaven. The word "He" seems to be used in a muddled and unclear way in this entire paragraph, unless you take into account the fact that HaShem, Yshu`a and the Ruach HaKodesh are in fact One. Since Messiah's purpose is to bring HaShem and mankind back together, the meaning of this phrase is that all of Heaven and Earth will work towards this reconciliation.

Bsorat – Hebrew for "good news." This term can apply to the four accounts of Messiah's Life or the entire body of Messianic Scripture.

Ruach HaKodesh – Holy Spirit

[11] * *In Whom also we were allotted the inheritance, previously chosen according to setting forth all things to work according to the volition of His will*, [12] *for those of us having previously trusted in Messiah to be a praise to His glory.* *

---

* 1:11-14 — The similarity between verses 13 & 14, and 11 & 12 is significant. Remembering the background of Rabbi Shaul, we remember that the Bible says that he was a student of Rabban Gamliel the Elder, Rosh Yeshiva of Beyt Hillel and grandson of Rabbi Hillel, founder of Beyt Hillel. This being the case, Rabbi Shaul was undoubtedly familiar with Rabbi Hillel's Seven Rules for interpreting the Torah. Shaul, is building one of them into his writing in this passage. He is using the Second Rule, G'zerah Shavah (Equivalence of expressions), to indicate an equality between the Messianic Jews and the Messianic non-Jews.

These two passages end with the same wording showing how both Jew and non-Jew can progress towards the same goal through Messiah. This passage rejects the theory of Dual-Covenant Theology. There is one set of Commandments for both Jew and Gentile, and one way to Heaven for both Jew and Gentile.

To clarify: The Commandments bring us closer to God in this life, and Messiah brings us to God in the next life. While both the Commandments and the Messiah have a similarity in function, they do not serve the same function and one cannot be traded for the other. Rabbi Shaul is establishing a sense of equality here in demonstrating that we are all working for HaShem, we all love Him and He loves all humanity.

* 1:11 — The words "all things" used here is true on multiple levels. Literally, in His omnipotence, God created the world in such a manner that His will is part of the natural order. Specifically, the Torah leads a person to a place where he is ready to accept Yshu`a as Messiah. Those Jews who accept Yshu`a as Messiah also feel lead even more strongly to obey God's commandments out of love for God, without thought of reward. This escalation in Torah observance also increases faith in Messiah.

* 1:11&12 — These verses describes the Jewish people. The Jewish people had faith that Messiah would come for many centuries, since the prophecy was first given in Genesis 49:10. This verse guarantees the inheritance of the Jewish people who follow Messiah. This passage also states that Messiah would be praised as the result of goodness that He grants the Jews who recognize and follow Him. This is of course a national, not individual selection, and many Jews chose not to be blessed in this manner.

Frequently, the Jewish people are referred to as "the Chosen People" without the speaker or audience pausing to discuss for what exact purpose were the Jewish people chosen. The Jewish people were chosen to be the vessel through which God brings mankind to Him. This is why the Torah and the Gospels are in such harmony. Of course one must truly study the full meaning of both the Torah and the Gospels to understand this fully.

13 _In Whom also, you, having heard the word of truth, the_
good news of the salvation of your [souls*], in Whom, also
believing, you were sealed with the promise of the Ruach
HaKodesh, 14 _Who is a guarantee of our inheritance until the_
redemption of salvation, [for you*] to be a praise to His
glory*.
*15 _Therefore hearing of the moral conviction among you in_
Adonai, Yshuà, and the love for the righteous people, 16 _I have_
not ceased giving thanks on your behalf, making mention in
my prayers, 17 _may Elohim, Adoneynu, Yshuà HaMashiach,_
Father of Glory*, give to you a spirit of wisdom and
revelation of knowledge of Him, 18 _having illuminated the eyes_

---

* 1:13 — The Greek Text literally translates as "the salvation of you." The use of the definite article, "the," indicates that the salvation spoken of is the most significant salvation that there is, spiritual salvation. This is a Hebraism wherein Rabbi Shaul uses Hebrew grammar, which is preserved in translation.

* 1:14 — The words "for you" are not really needed since they do not change the meaning of the sentence, but the length of the descriptive phrase referring to the Ruach HaKodesh is such that the sentence does not flow well. Specifically, the non-Jews were sealed to be a praise to the glory of God in His totality.

* 1:13&14 — These verses describe the non-Jews who come to know Messiah though hearing the words of Messianic Jewish Rabbis who spread the Message of Messiah. It also guarantees their inheritance and how Messiah would be praised as the result of

goodness that He grants the non-Jews who recognize and follow Him.

* 1:15-23 — Rabbi Shaul's use of the pronoun here seems vague unless you realize that the rabbi sees little difference between Abba (the Father), the Messiah, and the Ruach HaKodesh. In reading this paragraph one realizes that the word "He" applies to things done by God (the Father), by the Ruach HaKodesh, and by Yshu`a. Rabbi Shaul's understanding of the Shma (Deuteronomy 6:4) is that HaShem is a single unity. The Rabbi may not have been arrogant enough to think that he could understand and define HaShem, but it is obvious that he did not believe in dividing God into three separate people. The three aspects of God are united in a way that is beyond human comprehension but which is certainly real.

* 1:17 — This address for God uses proper names for God that literally translate as God, our God Yshu`a the Messiah, Father of Glory." This may seem longwinded, but in many common Hebrew prayers, God is referred to as "Adonai Eloheynu, King of the Universe." The usage here indicates Rabbi Shaul's understanding that there is only one God, and that for Messiah to be divine, He and the Father must be one. Yshu`a never told us to pray to Him, but only to the Father. Rabbi Shaul of course understood that if Messiah is divine then prayers directed to God would also be heard by all of the Godhead — Father, Messiah, and Spirit.

Ruach HaKodesh – The Holy Spirit

Adoneynu – Our God

of your mind* that you may know what the hope of His
calling is, and what the riches of the glory of His inheritance
among the sanctified are, 19 and what the surpassing greatness
of his power working in us who believe according to the power
of His strength, 20 which He worked in the Messiah raising
Him from the dead, and seating Him at His right hand* in
Heaven, 21 far above all rule and jurisdiction and power and
dominion and every name not only in This World, but also in
the World to Come, 22 *and all things subjected under His

---

* 1:18 — Science is based on observation and understanding. Since God is obvious in His creation, science has lead many brilliant peoples to believe in God. Since the entire Bible is true, and science is a search for truth, science if allowed to fully explore every question of reality would eventually come to the inescapable conclusion that God exists and that the Bible is completely true. Many Biblical facts are already proven by science. The rest will also be proven if mankind has enough time to investigate prior to Messiah's return.

* 1:20 — A prince who is His father's top general sits at the king's right hand while the queen sits at the king's left. Messiah is described in Joshua 5:14 as "שַׂר־צְבָא־יהוה (Sar Tzva Adonai)," which is, "the Prince of the Legion of Adonai." Messiah also stated in Matthew 13:40-43 that He would send His angels against those within the community of believers who teach against the Law.

* 1:22&23 — The εκκλησια (Ekkesia) referred to here is the Messianic Rabbinate or Beyt Din. The word

translated as "body" in many English translations was used very broadly in Greek both figuratively and literally. The word, "σωμα (soma)" always conveys a sense of wholeness or completeness. This is followed by the term "πληρωμα (pleroma)" which was a Greek proper noun. The Pleroma was the entire host of angels who mediate between HaShem and man. Since Messiah's function is to mediate between HaShem and mankind, this term conveys that meaning that Messiah controls and embodies all mediation between HaShem and man. This passage is very important to understand.

Rabbi Shaul's meaning from the Greek text is that the Messianic Rabbis of that time, many of whom were ordained by Yshu`a personally, served in all required functions and taught all correct doctrines of salvation and righteousness. A literal translation of the Greek of the latter part of verse 22 places the leader of the movement under Messiah's authority. It also uses the Greek word "κεφαλην (kephalen)," which means "head." This would translate the Hebrew title "Rosh" as in "Rosh Yeshiva," the leader of a Jewish seminary. Shaul is admitting, and rightfully so, that he has no authority to countermand anything taught by the Messiah and by extension anything in the Tanakh (Old Testament), since Yshu`a proclaimed the continuing authority of the Tanakh repeatedly throughout His ministry, notably Matthew 5:17-19. Over the centuries, people have occasionally used parts of Shaul's writings, taken out of context to argue against facts taught in the Tanakh and by Yshu`a Himself. Rabbi Kefa warned against this in Second Kefa 3:15&16.

feet, and he gave headship over all things to the Messianic
Beyt Din, 23 *which is his body, the completeness of all reality*
*with all things complete.**

2 1 *You had been dead* in the sins and guilty*
actions,* 2 *in which you then walked, according to the*
era of This World, according to the rulers of the

---

* 1:23 — Messiah being "the completeness of all reality with all things being complete" means that the world was not complete until God's plan for our salvation had been enacted physically, and that the Torah is not complete without Messiah.

* 2:1 — A person who has no relationship with HaShem or who has refused a relationship with HaShem may be physically alive, but spiritually they are dead. This is not because HaShem will send death to them, but because they have removed themselves from HaShem, the Source of All Life.

* 2:1— Rabbi Shaul is using the terminology found in Leviticus in the description of the Temple System. The Hebrew does not translate easily into either Greek or English. The word "**אשׁמו** (ashamo)," used to describe the Guilt Offering, can be either a noun or a verb, unlike the English word "guilt." From the context, we know the action is meant here. I used "guilty actions" in translation to make this easier to read. The word used for the Sin Offering is "**חטאת** (chatat)." Since the Temple System requires different Offerings for "sins" and for "guilts," even

though both actions are violations of God's Law, the difference must be important.

In this passage Rabbi Shaul demonstrates that he feels the difference is important even after Yshu`a gave His life for our sins and guilts. In the biblical sense, "sins" are violations that occur because the person does not know the Commandment in question, and "guilts" are sins that occur when the person is trying to do the right thing, but is overcome with temptation. There is a third form of violation of God's Law which is discussed in Number 15:30-31 which says that this third form is unforgivable and calls this "blasphemy against HaShem." In Bsorat Mattitiyahu 12:31&32, Yshu`a said that all violations are forgivable except "blasphemy against the Holy Spirit." This is what is spoken of in Numbers 15:30-31. So, Shaul excludes this from the list of sins previously performed by the converts since they had no knowledge of the quality of their old actions. [See Appendix Six for a more complete discussion of blasphemy against the Holy Spirit]

Bsorat Yochanan's reference to Messiah being the Word of God means that He is the living Torah. This means that the Temple system of Offerings can teach us a great deal about salvation through acceptance of Messiah. Rabbi Shaul is drawing from the Temple system in this passage.

Bsorat Mattitiyahu – the Gospel of Matthew

Bsorat Yochanan – The Gospel of John

powers of the air[*]*, the spirits currently working in the Sons of Rebellion*[*]*,* [3] *among whom we also conducted*

---

[*] 2:2 — The phrase "Ruler of the Powers of the Air" has been used by weak-minded and superstitious people to indicate that HaSatan has dominion over the air. A fictional demon was invented to embody this misconception.

Rabbi Shaul is using the term in the opposite way. Rabbi Shaul is pointing out that Pagan "gods" are all innately Satanic since they distract foolish people from worshiping HaShem, the Only Real God. He is also using "air" to indicate that these false religions are nothingness, sounds with no real substance or truth, what we in America frequently refer to as "hot air" namely a lot of bluster with nothing to back it up. His attitude is similar to that of Mosheh who told Pharaoh that Israel had to leave Egypt to worship HaShem because part of the worship was to "…kill the abominations (gods) of Egypt."

Rabbi Shaul knew that the Ephesian economy was based on the Pagan idols manufactured there and that the Messianic Believers were under great pressure to renounce HaShem or at least to contribute to the practice of idolatry. Idolatry is one of the three sins that a Follower of God must lay down his life rather than practice. So, the Rabbi made fun of the stupidity of idolatry, thereby following the Jewish understanding of the Commandment against idolatry. Fearing or hating idols just gives Idolaters a sense of power; so, the Rabbi subtly insults the idols, pointing out their impotence. Of course there were many cities in Asia Minor who depended upon idolatry for a great deal of their wealth, so this technique is applicable to a letter addressed to any of the congregations in any of those cities.

* 2:2 — This wording, "τοις Υιοις της Απειθειας(tois uiois tes apeitheias)," is a translation into Greek of a term used by Yshu`a Himself in Mattitiyahu 13:38. Yshu`a called those people who professed to be part of the Body of believers but who are actually servants of HaSatan, whether they know it or not, as "בני בליעל (Bnai B'liya`al)." The word "בני (Bnai)" means "sons [of]," and the word "בליעל (B'liya`al)" is a name for HaSatan. This name, B'liya`al, refers to HaSatan's character; it means "rebellious, lawless, and worthless." The double use of the definite article indicates that this is a proper name. This term is very significant in the specific notation of the concept of rebellion. Without the second use of the definite article, "apeitheias" could be translated as "disobedience," "disbelief" or "rebellion."

Rabbi Shaul, like any good Jew, knew that the human race began knowing God and then rebelled. All idolatry, Atheism, and evil stem from Adam's rebellion. Thus those who give themselves over to any sin are continuing Adam's rebellion. This term also brings to mind that a person is not damned for things that are not his fault; those who are damned deserve what they get. Of course, from what we know of the three types of sin (sins, guilts, and Blasphemies against the Holy Spirit), we know that some of how God judges us is subjective while the

ourselves — in the lusts of our flesh, doing the things desired by the flesh and the understandings [thereof], and were Children of Punishment as were all the rest.* *

[4] *But Elohim is abounding in mercy because of the greatness of His love with which he loved us* [5] *and, even though we were dead in our disobedience, He made us alive again by joining us with Messiah in His resurrection].* * *By chesed** *you are being saved,* [6] *and raised with Messiah and*

code of conduct is objective.

The terminology of this verse also brings up the differences between institutions and individuals. The parable of "the Wheat and the Tares" discusses evil people who are part of a good institution. But now, centuries later, we have man-made institutions within the good institution that Messiah established. The fragmentation between these groups is such that various denominations denounce others as "evil." Since the theologies of these various groups can be quite different and even oppose each other on a fundamental level, we cannot say that they are all "good," but this does not mean that there are not good people in all of them. Furthermore, while we are required to judge theologies, institutions, and potential courses of action, we must refrain from judging people.

* 2:3 — The term "Children of Punishment" indicates that humanity as a whole deserves punishment. All restraint of punishment is mercy from God.

* 2:3 — Here, the Rabbi reminds the entire congregation that we all begin as sinners and then come to an

understanding of HaShem. This is important to remember. If someone becomes self-righteous, they cannot reach anyone and frequently do not bother trying.

* 2:5a — The phrase "He made us alive again by joining us with Messiah [in His resurrection]" is translated here using the full definition of the word "συνεζωοποιησεν (sunesuopoinsen)," which means "to reanimate conjointly with," which, put simply, means that two things are linked and brought back to life together. The phrase "in His resurrection" is implied by the word and by the biblical event of Messiah's resurrection. It is added so that the casual reader understands the full implications of this verse.

* 2:5b — The Hebrew word "chesed" means "acts of kindness motivated only by love." The Greek word used "χαρις (karis)" means "gracious in manner and action especially as the result of divine influence." The Hebrew word very specifically describes how we are saved. See the Note on 1:2 for more details. It is also interesting to note that Rabbi Shaul indicates that our salvation is a continuing process and not a matter of saying a single prayer and becoming irrevocably saved no matter what evil a person may do after that.

seated in Heaven with Messiah, in Messiah, Yshuà, * 7 *to*
demonstrate in the ages that are coming the exceeding
abundance of His chesed, in goodness towards us in Messiah
Yshuà, 8 *because, by chesed you are saved through your*
moral conviction, but this is not from you, of Elohim is this
gift,
*9 *not by labor, lest anyone brag.* * 10 *For we are created by*
Him in Messiah Yshuà on the foundation of the Mitzvot, in

---

* 2:6 — The word "Messiah" is added into this verse with each use of the preposition "with" due to differences in Hebrew, Greek and English grammar. In English a preposition always needs an object even if the context makes the object obvious to the listener.

* 2:8 — We should be aware that while the moral conviction to follow Yshu`a is ours, the chesed is God's. Our chesed leads us to live in a godly manner, giving us the moral conviction to live according to God's will for us. However, even the most rigid obedience to all the Mitzvot (Commandments) of the Torah does not earn us a place in Heaven. When we look at the issue of salvation from an earthly perspective, it can be difficult to see how God gives us salvation as a gift and how we are still required to obey God's Mitzvot. Our natural inclination is to think that things are bought and paid for. However, Yshu`a did not teach us to accept Him for salvation and then commit evil actions.

God provided Yshu`a for our salvation and forgives us and brings us to Him out of love. Yshu`a taught us that we should love God so much that we desire to obey His Commandments as demonstrations of our love for Him. To people who see the Commandments as ways to express our love for God, they are not burdens, they are opportunities.

It can be difficult to understand how obedience to the Law does not give salvation while at the same time willful, arrogant, defiant, and remorseless violation of any Commandment can be blasphemy against the Holy Spirit, thus loosing us our salvation. This difficulty also comes from seeing things as commerce rather than a relationship. God loves us and He did not design the Commandments to provide salvation. The Commandments bless our lives, they give us better understanding of Yshu`a, and they bring us closer to God in this life. Salvation is a love relationship. God loves us and wants us to love him enough to desire to please Him. [See Appendix Six for a more complete discussion of blasphemy against the Holy Spirit]

* 2:9 — Salvation is not earned. Salvation has always been a function of HaShem's Chesed, His act of Mercy that is only motivated by His love for us. The Mitzvot are wonderful expressions of HaShem's love for us, and obeying these Mitzvot is the best way to express our love for Him, but that it not the way to Heaven, it is just a thing that godly people do on their way to Heaven. The individual must still make a conscious choice to accept Yshu`a as Messiah and Savior.

*which Elohim had already ordained for us to walk.**
11 *Therefore, remember you were Goyim in the flesh —*
those called "Uncircumcised" by those who are called
"Circumcised" whose flesh was made so by hand, 12 *that you*
were at that time without Messiah, having been alienated
from the community of Israel, and strangers to the promise of
*the Covenant, hopeless and godless in the world.**
13 *But now, in Messiah, Yshuà, you, those who were far*
off, became near by the blood of Messiah, 14 *for He himself is*
our peace — making both one, having broken the Middle

---

* 2:10 — God created the world for us to live good lives free of any sin. God defined what is good and what is evil before He created the Earth. This definition is the 613 Mitzvot found in the Torah. Man chose to sin instead doing what he was created to do. However, the preparations were made when the world was created for us to live lives free from sin.

The "meaning of Life" that secular philosophers have sought for millennia, is stated in Ecclesiastes 12:13&14, "*Let us hear with understanding the conclusion of the entire Word: Revere Elohim, and preserve and observe His Commandments, because of this is everyone [created]. Because Elohim will bring every action to judgment with all that is hidden, if good or if evil.*" The Hebrew phrase that translates as, "because of this is everyone," means that this is the reason for which we exist, in other words: "the Meaning of Life."

In Deuteronomy 30:11-14, HaShem makes it clear that he has made it possible to uphold His Word. This is exactly what we would expect if it is the purpose of creation. But the fact that it is possible to obey the Commandments causes many people a great deal of embarrassment. Because of this man-made theologies have been established to obscure the fact that we can actually obey God.

Of course, since salvation is never promised as a reward for obedience to the Commandments, we still need Yshu`a for salvation. There is only one way for anyone to be saved; Yshu`a said, "No one comes to the Father except through Me."

* 2:11&12 — In these verses, Rabbi Shaul is not discounting the value of Circumcision, his reference is to those people of Jewish descent who would shun a non-Jew rather than show that person the goodness of HaShem. The Jews were chosen to be the FIRST people who came to HaShem, not the ONLY people who came to Him. The Jewish people were given a mission to be a "Nation of Kohanim," a Nation of Priests, but many had chosen not to bother with the non-Jews.

In verse 11, the word "ethnos," which translates as "foreign nationals" is used. The context here, due to their former paganism, equates to the very worst definitions of "goyim." It should also be noted that the past tense here indicates that they have not only accepted Messiah, but also cast off their old culture and ethnicity. This equates the "grafting into the Olive Tree" that Rabbi Shaul wrote of in his letter to the Romans.

* 2:14 — The phrase "Middle Wall of Partition" literally translates the Hebrew word "m'chitzah," which is the partition in an Orthodox synagogue that separates the men from the women. In this case there is an obvious reference to the wall in the Temple, separating the Gerim from the native born Jews. Combining the two meanings gives us a clear picture that there should be no separation in the Messianic synagogues between those people who were born Jewish and those who were not born Jewish.

* 2:15 — Translation of this verse has been problematic for many people. The syntax (grammatically correct word order) of Greek is different from that of English or Hebrew. Because some English words have no equivalent in Greek or Hebrew, and vice versa, translators need to add words to make the translated words into a sentence that has meaning.

The problem with most translations of this verse is that translators chose words that would make the verse agree with their own denominational theology, rather than making the verse agree with what the Messiah said Himself or the rest of the paragraph. By doing this they cause their translation to disagree with the intent of Rabbi Shaul, and with the Greek text. Some of the words chosen by translators are words that have no equivalents in Greek or Hebrew and therefore are not appropriate. In this case, the words "of" and "to" are implied in the Greek text even though English grammar requires them. Other translators have chosen to add words that translate Greek words found in other verses of the Greek texts but not in this verse; the addition of those words does not render an accurate translation and actually deviates from the translational standards that those translators set themselves.

This translation uses the word "to" referring to opposition directed towards the Law of God by man's fleshly desires. Throughout history, people have come to the Jewish people seeking God, but have been opposed to the idea of obeying God's Laws.

Most of these people oppose the idea of obeying God's Laws without even knowing what the Law entails; they blindly rebel against the concept of the Law. This attitude had for centuries kept many Gentiles from devoting themselves to God to the fullest extent of their ability. But in Messiah's life, we see that He obeyed all of the Law thus giving us the proof that God is not a hypocrite, that He obeys his own Laws. This makes God seem far less tyrannical than He might seem in the eyes of those who do not know Him yet.

The meaning of the verse is that Messiah destroys the hostility that all men, Jew and Gentile, have towards obeying the Word of God and thus unites all Believers in one new people. The wording here uses "ανθρωπον (anthropon)," which means, "man" to describe this new people. This brings to mind the Talmud's assertion that Jews are "adam" (a man). According to this Talmud passage, only Jews and Gerim (converts to Judaism) are "adam;" pagans are "`amim," peoples. While anti-Semites have claimed that this means that the Talmud calls non-Jews

opposition to the Torah, with its Commandments in Chukim, the two, He molds into one new people, making peace, [16] and reconciling both in one body to Elohim through the stake, killing the hostility in Himself.**

[17] Also, coming, He proclaimed "Peace, peace for the far and for the near," [18] because through Him, we both have

---

"non-human," this is not the meaning of the text. The Talmudic assertion is that all Jews are united in a common destiny as if we were all one person. The Messianic Scriptures convey this same idea, but are much more direct with stating the inclusion of non-Jews who come to know God.

* 2:14 — The Greek word "Δογμασιν (Dogmasin)" translates the Hebrew word "חֻקִּים (Chukim)," which is the proper noun naming one of the three groups of Mitzvot. The three groups are Mishpatim, Edot and Chukim. The Mishpatim are those Commandments that are absolutely mandatory for a healthy human society. The Edot are the Remembrances that strengthen our faith. The Chukim spoken of in this verse are those commandments that God does not explain and for which we do not see a reason except that God commanded them and we love God enough to obey Him.

Because it is not easy to see a relevance of the Chukim, they are the Commandments that we are first tempted to violate. These are the commandments that we are most likely to violate first, but once we start down the road of evil it is easy to continue by committing actions that are evil and increasingly obvious as being evil. So we must be vigilant in protecting our souls from any sin even those that come from violating Mitzvot that we do not understand. Our gratitude for what Messiah has done for us should overcome the automatic desire to disobey a command or commandment that we do not understand.

* 2:16 — The close of this paragraph makes it clear that the translation of 2:15 should read as rendered above, that Messiah destroyed man's opposition to God's Word. Again Shaul uses one of Rabbi Hillel's Seven Rules for Interpreting Torah. This time, the Third Rule, "Binyan av" or as Rabbi Ishmael ben Eliezer clarified, Binyan av mikatuv echad (Building up a "family" from a single text). In this single passage he says the same thing with similar, but not identical, wording twice, so that the two verses in the passage provide built-in error checking to prevent misinterpretation.

Additionally, we should also see that Messiah's suffering on our behalf is something for which we should be devoutly grateful; we should be grateful to the point of obeying God as an expression of our gratitude. Therefore the resistance that the Gentiles felt at accepting God's Law is overcome by their new-found gratitude to Him.

access to the Father in one spirit. *
[19] *Therefore, certainly, you are no longer strangers and*
aliens, but fellow citizens of Elohim's People and of the House
of Elohim, * [20] *having built upon the foundation of the*
*representatives** *and the Prophets, the cornerstone being the*

---

* 2:17&18 — Part of this passage is quotation from Isaiah 57:19. The quote is significant in more than just the wording; it carries the context of Isaiah 57:15-21 forward to this passage. The passage from Isaiah foretells God's eventual forgiveness of the past sins of those who turn away from sin and towards Him. It also tells that those who refuse to turn from evil will have no peace.

Additionally, the full passage in Isaiah says that God will accomplish this. Therefore this is another instance of Shaul indicating that Messiah is divine. Another important understanding of the wording is that the passage in Isaiah uses a variant of the same word used in Numbers 9:10, concerning the Second Passover for someone who was on "a distant road." The word is understood to mean either physically far away or spiritually far away. So this is yet another reference to the unity of those who actually follow Messiah and His teaching of the Torah regardless of lineage.

Translational note: since this passage is a translation into Greek of the Hebrew text of Isaiah 57:19, this translation uses the original source.

* 2:19 — Rabbi Shaul states that the Native Jew and the Convert to Messianic Judaism are equals in a single community. This is a reference to the same ideas that Rabbi Shaul discusses in Romans, chapter 11. This passage gives the Gentile converts to Messianic Judaism the same status as the Torah gives to the convert to Judaism. While this agrees with the Torah, it seems to contradict what Rabbi Shaul wrote in First Corinthians 7:17. Since we know that truth does not contradict truth, a more thorough reading of the passage in First Corinthians in required. "*To each as God had divided — each as Adonai has called Him, so let him walk. This in all the congregations, I institute.*" So, this anti-conversion ruling was of man-made origin.

This being the case, we must also consider that this ruling is not sent in Rabbi Shaul's letters to all the congregations, but only to the congregations in Corinth, whereas this letter was sent across Asia Minor. This leads one to believe that Rabbi Shaul did not intend to rebuild the Middle Wall that Messiah tore down, but rather was addressing specific conditions in the city of Corinth. As such, there is no real conflict. The term "House of Elohim" is also very important. This indicated that the practice of Torah observance taught by Yshu`a is taught by God. Of course, those people who believe in the divinity of Messiah understand that He taught the Torah, and that in Yshu`a doing so, Elohim taught the Torah.

* 2:20 — See note to 1:1a concerning the original meaning of the Greek word "αποστολος (apostolos)."

Messiah, Yshuà, Himself, * [21] *in whom, all the building is fitted together, and grows into a Holy Temple in Adonai,* [22]*in whom, you are being built together into the House of Elohim in spirit!* *

---

* 2:20 — Rabbi Shaul makes it clear that these non-Jewish Followers of Messiah are part of Judaism not because the Rabbi says so, but because they adhere to the precepts, customs, and beliefs of Judaism with Messiah central to their faith. Their status as part of the Community of Israel is something that they have earned in accordance with the Law and with the blessing of Messiah. The word "foundation" refers to Judaism, specifically Judaism as Yshu`a interpreted it, which for the most part agrees with Beyt Hillel the Rabbinical group that played the greatest part in forming modern Orthodox Judaism.

* 2:21&22 — The Talmud teaches that in the Messianic Era our Offerings will consist of prayers and praise (Talmud Bavli, Pesikta 79a). This being the case, we ourselves become the Temple when we dedicate ourselves to Him and seek His will in our lives. From a linguistic and poetic standpoint, the subtleties here give us additional information when placed within their historical and cultural context.

Messiah came to teach the correct way of interpreting the Torah to the Jews. He primarily taught to Pharisaic Jews since Sadducaic Jews did not believe that there was an afterlife, thus the concept of salvation from damnation was outside their belief system. The Pharisaic Jews were divided into many schools of thought. These schools of thought were called "houses." Notable examples are "Beyt Hillel (House of Hillel)" and "Beyt Shammai (House of Shammai)."

The terminology here not only places the Followers of Yshu`a into the realm of Judaism, it also expresses the idea that the Messianic Community follows God. We also see that the term which would be best translated as "Beyt Elohim" when compared to Matthew, chapter 23, further indicates Rabbi Shaul's belief in the divinity of the Messiah. This indicates that the practice of Torah observance taught by Yshu`a is taught by God. Of course, those people who believe in the divinity of Messiah understand that He taught the Torah and that in Yshu`a doing so, Elohim taught the Torah.

The knowledge that Messiah is divine could lead someone into the sin of "Messiah-worship." This is a form of idolatry in which the sinner takes one aspect of God and elevates it above the rest of God's totality sometimes to the exclusion of the rest of God. This form of idolatry distorts and redefines "god" into a false definition that becomes an idol of ideas rather than an idol of stone metal or wood, but an idol all the same. This term, however, would also lead one away from worshiping Messiah, since "Elohim" refers to the totality of God. Many people who commit Messiah-worship use the divinity of Messiah or the Unity of the Divine to excuse the practice of praying to Messiah, and worshiping Messiah. Their excuses do not outweigh the words of Messiah. Yshu`a Himself commanded us to worship and pray only to HaShem, the Father, in Matthew 6:9-13.

3 1 Because of this, I, Shaul, prisoner of Messiah, Yshuà,
on behalf of you, the Gerim. * 2 Surely, you have heard of the
chesed of Elohim, given to me, 3 so that by way of revelation
was made known to me the mystery as I wrote before in brief,
4 reading about which, you are able to understand my
knowledge of the mystery of Messiah, 5 which in other
generations was not made known to the sons of men as in the
manner that it has now been revealed to His representatives
and prophets in the Spirit: 6 the Gerim are co-heirs, and parts
of the same body, and co-participants of His promise in
Messiah through HaBsorat*.*

---

* 3:1-13 — Rabbi Shaul teaches that the reason that the Jews failed in their early attempts to allow non-Jews to convert to Judaism and join with the Jewish Community was that this union, while possible for a few individuals, would not be possible for the non-Jews en masse until Messiah made it possible. The secrecy that Rabbi Shaul speaks of may have been a lack of human understanding, or it may have been an actual secrecy in HaShem's planning the salvation of the non-Jews. However, these two ideas are both speculative and irrelevant to our understanding. The simple fact is that mankind did not know how HaShem planed to reconcile Jew and non-Jew until He set forth His plan through Messiah. Because the truth does not change, there were hints in the Torah. Commandments were given that apply to the non-Jews who come to know God. Rather than becoming obsolete in light of Messiah's coming, these parts of the Torah gain a more complete meaning since only now can they be fully implemented.

* 3:1 — Rabbi Shaul remains mindful of his service to God, and sees all hardships that result from his dedication as part of His service, thereby making these hardships easier to endure. Many "Christian scholars" claim that Ephesians was written circa 80 CE by someone other than Rabbi Shaul. These "scholars" claim that this mystery-writer was probably one of his students. However, this verse identifies the author as Rabbi Shaul. Furthermore, in First Thessalonians 2:3-5, Rabbi Shaul taught against using any deceit in any service to HaShem; so, it is doubtful that any student of his would lie about his identity. It is also likely that Rabbi Shaul literally was a prisoner when he wrote this. There are more references to his incarceration in 4:1, 4:7-11, and 6:20.

Translational Note: the Greek word "ethnos" appears here, but the context clearly indicates that he is referring to people who were not physically descended from Avrham, Yitzchak and Ya`akov, but who have come to know God through Messianic Judaism.

* 3:6— The Hebrew word "bsorat" means "good news." The definite article, "ha," makes this a specific good news, namely the good news of Messiah's coming. The Hebrew term, "HaBsorat," is used here because these people were taught a Jewish Message of Messiah. While people were not coerced into taking on all of the Torah at once, they were part of a Jewish faith and went to Jewish synagogues where the rabbis knew and taught that Yshu`a is the Messiah.

7 I became a messenger of this [HaBsorat] according to the
gift of Elohim's chesed, given to me according to the work of
His power. 8 To me, the least the Blessed Ones*, was given this
chesed: to announce among the Gerim the unimaginable
vastness of the blessings of the Messiah, 9 and to bring to light
all that is the partnership of the mystery that was hidden
from the ages in Elohim, Who created all things, 10 that can
now be known to the principalities and authorities in Heaven,
through the Messianic Rabbinate, the diverse wisdom of
Elohim, 11 according to the purpose of the ages which He made
in Messiah, Yshuà, Adonaynu, * 12 in whom, we have boldness
and access in confidence [to Elohim], through His moral
conviction. 13 Therefore, I ask you not to be weak as a result
of my troubles on your behalf which is your glory*.

---

* 3:8 — The "Blessed Ones" here could be translated two ways either as "sanctified ones" meaning all who have accepted Messiah and are saved and made holy though His blessing, or as "Blessed Ones" referring to the Disciples who were blessed by Yshu`a. Since Rabbi Shaul was not given to false modesty, the former interpretation is easily ruled out. This also agrees with the reference in 3:10 below. Rabbi Shaul refers to himself as the "least" of the Messianic leaders because only he had never sat at the feet of Messiah in Yshu`a's physical lifetime. While Rabbis Ya`akov ben Yosef and Yhudah ben Yosef did not walk with Him during His three and one half year ministry, it is almost certain that they did study Torah with Him at home for years prior to His ministry.

* 3:10a — The word translated as "principalities" refers to the Arch Angels and the word translated as

"authorities" translates as an order just below the Arch Angels. Since angel worship is a form of idolatry specifically mentioned in HaBsorat, it is best to recognize that this verse indicates that God's relationship with the leaders of the Messianic movement is more important to the people than the people's relationship with various angels.

* 3:10b — God's plan for humanity specifically the inclusion of the Gerim was first revealed to the leaders of the Messianic movement. We see this earlier, in Acts chapter 10, when Rabbi Kefa is given the vision that all people, regardless of origin may be saved through Yshu`a, and enter into the Community of Israel. As God worked among the Messianic community, through the Messianic Rabbinate, the Messianic Jew, the Messianic Ger and the angels all learned God's plan for uniting all who place their trust in Yshu`a Ha Mashiach.

* 3:11 — The English words "our Lord" are frequently used to translate the Greek "Kurio hemon," but this hides the fact that a proper name is used here which has been translated into Greek. "Adoneynu" is Hebrew for "our Lord," but it is a proper name for God the Father. It's use in this context demonstrates again that Rabbi Shaul saw God as one unity.

* 3:13 — The term "your glory" does not refer to secular glory, but rather to heavenly glory. In this case it refers to people accepting God and Messiah and learning to live godly lives. Glory means "deserving of praise," and the highest praise given to anyone in the Bible is that they were Torah observant.

*[14] * By reason of this, I bend my knees to the Father, [15] from whom every family in Heaven and on Earth is named. * [16] So that He may give to you from the abundance of His glory to become strength by the power of His Spirit within your inner being, [17] so that the Messiah may dwell in your hearts through your moral conviction, in love being rooted and settled, [18] so that you, will be strengthened to comprehend, with all the*

---

* 3:14-21 — Rabbi Shaul's well wishing here is somewhat uncharacteristic, but this may be because he does not believe that he will have an opportunity to contact the recipients of this letter again. It is possible that this was his farewell letter just prior to his execution. His concern that our faith be based on our love for God and be blessed by Messiah's love for us is reminiscent of the Shma and the Vahavta (Deuteronomy 6:4-9) which are the core of Judaism. Some textual critics believe that this is the end of one letter and that 4:1 begins a second letter. Their theory is that the two letters were cobbled together later. Based upon the beginning of Chapter Four, it seems more likely that Rabbi Shaul wrote this letter in two sittings and that this is a break between sittings.

* 3:15 — This verse refers to the idea that HaShem created all nations at the Tower of Bavel. Noting that the Greek word "πατρια (patria)" refers to descent from founding fathers of bloodlines makes it easier to see this reference to the divergent nationalities that began with God splitting the people into various nations at the Tower of Bavel. It is also in keeping with the all-inclusive tone of this letter. Shaul

reminds us that humanity was created as a single people and that God split us into separate nations.

This also hints that through God, and only through God, mankind can be reunited. By mentioning the biblical fact that HaShem created the non-Jewish nations, Rabbi Shaul is attempting to refute the idea that non-Jews are inferior. Ironically, It is the non-Jews who adopt this false idea and then seek to make themselves "Jewish" by erroneous, man-made theologies or customs. This particular manifestation of low self-esteem has lead many believers to accept false theologies and to even renounce Messiah Himself in their misguided attempts to become "more Jewish."

Anti-Missionaries in Asia Minor capitalized on this psychology to lead many non-Jewish followers of Messiah away from belief in Messiah and into non-Messianic branches of Judaism. This same tactic is still effective today. Ironically, the fact is that rejecting the Jewish Messiah does not make anyone "more Jewish;" if anything, they become "less Jewish."

It should also be noted that within the Modern Messianic Community, some Gentiles makes accusations of "elitism" based on their own feelings of jealousy and not upon the actions of Messianic Jews. Almost all Messianic Jews observe God's commandment to respect the Messianic Gerim - those Gentiles who adopt a Biblical (Jewish) lifestyle as part of the faith in Messiah. [Note for further explanation see Appendix Seven: Biblical Conversion: Gentiles are not Goyim]

Sanctified Ones, the width, and the length, and the depth, and the height,* [19] *to know the knowledge that goes beyond the normal boundaries of knowledge* of Messiah's love, so that you may be filled to all the fullness of Elohim*.*

---

* 3:18 — "Sanctified Ones" as used here, refers to all people, both Jewish and non-Jewish, who accept Yshu`a as Messiah.

* 3:19a — Through the Holy Spirit we know Messiah's love for us in a way that is beyond normal knowledge. A person who does not know Messiah cannot understand His love for us or even understand how a love that vast could exist.

* 3:19b — Once we comprehend Messiah's love for us, we are able to be filled with all the blessings that God has given us. Our natural response to Messiah's love is to love Him back and our love for Him brings us into a fuller relationship with God. In the Jewish mindset, the Mitzvot are blessings that God has given us to bring us closer to Him, and to show His love for us.

Yshu`a taught that our observance of the Mitzvot must be done with the correct kavanah. This makes our observance stricter, but also ensures that our obedience to HaShem has the correct effect on our souls. Yshu`a spent three and a half years teaching the Torah, showing His followers the correct way to observe the Commandments.

Of course, in cases where the Pharisaic rabbis of his time were in agreement with each other and correct in their interpretation He did not have to say anything to correct them. Therefore, even the silence of HaBsorat on an issue teaches us a great deal.

So, being "filled with the Fullness of Elohim" means that now we have a clearer idea of the correct mechanics of Torah observance and of the spirituality of Torah observance. As such, observance of the Mitzvot becomes even more important to the Messianic Gerim and Messianic Jews than ever before because now that that have been completed by Messiah we can observe them correctly. We also have even greater motivation to obey the Mitzvot now that we know what Yshu`a has done for us.

HaBsorat – the four Gospels. Sometimes also used to refer to the Messianic Scriptures as a whole or to the general message of Yshu`a HaMashiach.

Kavanah – (Heb. "intention") the motivation that causes us to perform the actions we perform. In this case, our motivations for obeying God.

Mitzvot – The 613 Commandments found in the Bible.

Pharisaic – referring to the sect of Judaism, and all its various sub-sects, that are defined by two basic theological beliefs: 1, That there is an afterlife; 2, that each person must strive to be righteous instead of simply "buying off" God with offerings. Yshu`a taught that these two beliefs were correct.

[20] *And to Him who is beyond able to do all things, to accomplish more than we ask or imagine,* [21] *His is the glory in the Messianic Rabbinate in the Messiah Yshuà to all generations of the era of the eras**. *Amen**.

4 [1] *Therefore I, the prisoner in Adonai, implore walk in with all modesty and humility, with patience, upholding** *each other in love,* [3] *being eager to preserve the unity of the Spirit in the bond of peace.** [4] **One body and one Spirit, just*

---

* 3:21a — It is the responsibility of the Messianic Rabbinate to glorify God and to teach the Word of Messiah to the generation of that era and all subsequent eras. Also we must remember that all true glory belongs to God. A teacher of Scripture, no matter how skilled, no matter how blessed with ability, can never improve upon God's Word. Therefore, the Messianic Rabbinate openly gave all praise and credit for goodness, all glory, to God.

* 3:21b — At first this wording may seem strange. We commonly think of a "Messianic Era" without realizing that this era is composed of four distinct eras. First, there was the "Era of the Talmidim," when Rabbis who were taught By Yshu`a Himself and by those whom the original Talmidim taught. Second, there was the "Era of the Gentiles" when Christian churches spread the word of Messiah across the globe. Then the Era of the "Messianic Synagogue" began. In this era, the Messianic synagogues are restoring a "Whole-Bible" understanding of Yshu`a's teachings. Fourth, eventually, the Last Days will come.

* 4:2 — The Greek text uses "ανεχομενοι (anekomenoi)," which means, "to hold oneself up against." This is used in the same manner as "עֵזֶר כְּנֶגְדּוֹ (`ezer k'gedo), which means "a helper against him," is used in Genesis 2:18. Eve was to be a helper against Adam in that she was to help him overcome his personal desires that conflicted with the Law of God. The same applied to Adam helping Eve. Men and women inherently possess different strengths and weaknesses; thus in a marriage both the husband and the wife can lead his or her strength to the other when needed. Rabbi Shaul applies this same working concept to the congregation. People can help each other resist temptation.

* 4:2&3 — Here Rabbi Shaul is not summing up the entire Law; he is listing some character traits that help a person to obey Messiah's injunction to keep the Law in spirit as well as in flesh. This is an extension of the technique that Messiah taught in Matthew 5:1-16. Basically, if one cultivates at all times the character traits that oppose temptation, it becomes easier to resist temptation when it arises. Shaul is specifically focusing on those traits that not only lead us to obey Commandments, but also help promote unity within a congregation or community. This is a logical focus for him since he is attempting to ensure the survival of the Messianic congregation after his death and the eventual deaths of all the Disciples. A good spiritual leader works to focus the devotion of his congregants on God not on himself.

Talmidim – Hebrew for "students." In this case those who were taught by Yshu`a and those taught by the original students of Yshu`a.

as you were called you were called in one hope of your calling,
[5] *one Rebe*, one moral conviction, one immersion*,* [6] *and one*
Elohim, the Father of all, El Shaddai.* [7] *To each one of us*
was given chesed to the measure of the gift of Messiah.
[8]*Therefore it says,*

> *"You went up on high*
> *You have led the exiles captive,*
> *You took gifts of man." **

---

* 4:5 — This verse does not mean that a person can only be immersed once in his or her life. Obviously, that would be a violation of God's Law. It does mean that only an immersion that is done with understanding that Yshu`a is the Messiah has spiritual benefit. Additionally, this goes back to the concept of the anti-missionaries trying to convert people to non-Messianic Judaism. Conversion to Judaism is done primarily though the act of immersion. So, Shaul is also stating that conversion away from Messianic Judaism is not a valid action. The term actually indicates that the immersion for a Jew who accepts Yshu`a as Messiah is the same as the immersion of a non-Jew who accepts Yshu`a as Messiah.

* 4:6 — The Hebrew name of God, El Shaddai does not translate directly into any other language. Typically "All-Significant" is used in English. However, the meaning is, "all powerful, all important, omnipresent, and omniscient." The Greek text here tries to approximate that in Greek by literally reading, "above all, and through all, and in all." Since the translation fails it is only fitting that we revert to the

actual name approximated by the Greek text. This name of God that is usually reserved for times when he is doing miracles. It has been noted that the unification of Jews and Gentiles is miraculous.

* 4:7&8 - Rabbi Shaul references Psalm 68:19 (68:18 in the Christian Bible), which refers to the ultimate redemption of Israel and what Messiah will do upon His return. It also seems that he is attempting to mirror Messiah's self sacrifice at least in his emotions by consoling himself that his imprisonment is the result of actions taken on the behalf of those people to whom he is writing. Obviously, a man like Shaul would be comforted by the fact that his impending execution is the result of serving God in a manner that emulated the actions of Yshu`a Himself.

*4:9-11 — Verses 4:9-11 are a Midrash. Rabbi Shaul is building his allegory upon the verses from Psalm 68. In verse 10, he interprets the phrase "led the exiles captive" as having freed the believers from the captivity of sin and given them a new mission and a new role in life. This new mission is a captivity of a joyous, godly nature. This allegory may also be another reference to the Rabbi's own earthly captivity.

* 9 Now, "You went up," what is it unless He also went
down into the lower parts of the earth?* 10 He coming down is
also He coming up up, far above all the heavens, so that He
could complete all things. 11 And He provided some
representatives, and some prophets, and some evangelists, and
some shepherds and rabbis* 12 for the maturing of the
Sanctified People, for the work of ministry to build the body
of the Messiah, 13 until we all attain unity of moral conviction
and the knowledge of the Son of Elohim, to a man fully

---

* 4:9 — This section that reads as, "the lower parts of the earth?" refers to She`ol, where those who had died awaited Messiah's resurrection. This touches on pre-Messiah Jewish Cosmology. Specifically, no one could be in Gan Eden (Heaven) or Geyhinnom (Hell) until Judgement which in turn could not happen until they had the opportunity to accept salvation.

Sheol is described as being in the earth and having two compartments, one for those whom God knows will accept salvation and one from those whom He knows will reject Yshu`a. Each compartment is a shadow of what lies ahead for the souls therein. This makes the choice of those who decided to reject Yshu`a even more ridiculous since they knew the alternative.

It also shows God extending a second chance for salvation to people who did not deserve it. Many people have complained that God is not "fair." While this is true, what they fail to see is that He is more merciful and loving than "fairness" would allow. We should be thankful that God is better, kinder, more merciful, and more loving than simple fairness would allow.

* 4:11 — The question arises from this verse as to whether or not a Rabbi should be both Shepherd and Teacher to his flock. Some translators combine the Greek words which are translated as "Shepherds" and as rabbis" in this verse to "Shepherd-teachers." This is not entirely correct. The word translated as "rabbis" is "διδασκαλους (didaskalous)," which means "doctor, master, or teacher." Since we know that Rabbi Shaul is not advocating violating Messiah's injunction against using the title "rebe (master)," we can rule out the "master" definition. Actually, a combination of the remaining two is more likely. This would be an expert (doctor) of teaching. This combination also translates best as "rabbis" rather than the English word "teachers."

In this context, it can also refer to Yeshiva Instructors, experts who train rabbis. A rabbi today must be a shepherd to his flock, which includes teaching them and comforting them. And teachers should take the time to ensure that what they teach is biblically accurate. The most probable understanding here is that both things are meant simultaneously. For the shepherd to truly minister to his congregation he must teach them the truth from the Bible. Common practice today is to accept the interpretation that a denomination publishes without doing personal research, but the Bible both in the Torah and in the Messianic Scriptures places the responsibility upon the man who actually delivers the words to the people.

formed to the measure of the stature of the completeness of Messiah,[*] [14*]*that we may no longer be small children being blown about and carried away by every wind of doctrine, by the schemes of man in trickery in the trap of error.*[*] [15]*Instead, telling the truth in love, we may grow in all things into Him who is the head, Messiah,* [16] *by whom all of the body is being fitted together and united through every bond supplied according to the working in the measure of each part, producing the growth of the body, building itself up in love.*

[*17] *Therefore, I say this, and attest in Adonai: no longer*

---

[*] 4:13 — This unity of moral conviction has not yet occurred within the body of Messiah. In the Age of the Gentiles, the message of Messiah was carried across the globe. All people over all the earth have had the opportunity to accept or reject the Message of Messiah. Now, we see a growing number of non-Jewish believers in Messiah seeking a greater unity with the Jewish Followers of Messiah. These non-Jews want to know how the Disciples worshiped God and they are growing to the same moral conviction: all of the Bible is true; none of it was defective and therefore none was abolished. The Disciples knew that fulfilling the Law meant adding the additional requirement that a person be motivated by love for God and a genuine desire to please God. The process will not be complete until Messiah returns, but the Body of Believers is coming closer to that goal than it has in centuries.

[*] 4:14-16 — This passage goes back to verse 11. If every individual teacher in the entire body of Bible-teachers takes personal responsibility for ensuring

that what he teaches agrees with all of the Bible not simply an interpretation of a single verse taken out of context, then a single erroneous person, no matter how eloquent cannot introduce false doctrines. Rabbi Shaul addressed the issue of false theologies being wormed into the congregations in Second Thessalonians, chapter two, where he labels Antinomianism as the theology of Armillus (whom Christians call "the Anti-Christ"). Nearly two thousand years later Believers in Messiah have come in contact with many other pagan worship practices and theologies. Some of these have been assimilated despite Shaul's warnings and the Bible's prohibition against using pagan practices in attempts to worship God. This prohibition is found in Deuteronomy 12:29-32.

* 4:14 — The phrase "trap of error" is closer to the Greek text and conveys a meaning that is lost on many people. Error, even when we have been lied to still leads us into evil. If we violate the Commandments, even without evil intent, our actions are still evil. The most insidious tactic of HaSatan is to tell us that evil actions are now permissible. This is the theology Rabbis Shaul identifies with Armillus (the anti-Messiah) in Second Thessalonians, chapter two, and it encourages the person to blaspheme against the Holy Spirit without even realizing what they have done.

* 4:17-24 — Rabbi Shaul discusses the basis for the immorality in Paganism and the fundamental errors inherent in Paganism as well the fact that the lies and errors of Paganism must be completely rejected by those who accept Messiah.

will you walk as the Gentiles walk, in the vanity of their minds, [18] having been darkened in intellect, being alienated from the life of Elohim, through the ignorance in them, which results from the callous stupidity of their hearts, [19] who having rejected joy,* give themselves up to lust, to working all uncleanness with greediness. [20] But you learned the complete opposite of that: Messiah! [21] In fact, you heard Him and were taught about Him, that the truth in Yshuà is:* [22] cast off of you the former behavior of the old man, corrupted through*

---

* 4:18 — The Greek word "πωρωσιν (porosin)" has two meanings "callousness" and "stupidity." From the context, it is easy to see that both are meant here. The Pagans are stupid because they do not allow God's truth to penetrate into them.

Today people try to be politically correct and tip-toe around the feelings of people whom they believe to be wrong. Rabbi Shaul obviously did not suffer from that inhibition. He told the truth whether people wanted to hear it or not. Of course, that level of dedication did get him executed by the Romans.

* 4:19 — Judaism teaches that all joy and happiness come from God. A corrupt person may be entertained by sinful actions, but the corrupt person will never become happy though his evil actions.

* 4:21 — A concept of Judaism that does not carry forward into multi-cultural secular societies is that the Bible is true. It is not simply a source for moral or philosophical truths, but it is actually factual. Some parts are poetically or metaphorically written, but the intended meaning is factual. This is why there is no

name for “Judaism” in the Bible. The study of Physics, Chemistry, Biology, and Torah are all considered studies of reality. There are names for sub-groups of Judaism, but not for Judaism as a whole. The Bible is reality. People have interpretations for parts of it and those interpretations require names so that they can be discussed. To give an example: we have no name for people who believe that fire is hot because it is an undeniable fact. The Bible is seen much the same way in Judaism.

The leaders of the Early Messianic Movement did not depart from Judaism; they departed from some of the man-made additions to Judaism. There is significant evidence in the Messianic Scriptures to indicate that some additions which non-Messianic Rabbis believed to be implied by the Bible were retained in the Messianic synagogues of the First Century CE.

The Early Messianic Movement was referred to as the “ההליכה HaHalakha” in Hebrew, or οδου (Hodos)” in Greek. HaHalakha means “the Walk,” “The Manner,” or, by extension, “the Walkway” or “Path.” In non-Messianic Judaism, Halakhah is the study of how to apply the Commandments to our lives. By specifying “The Walk,” the Disciples referred to the lifestyle and interpretation of the Torah taught by Yshu`a. The Greek word has multiple meanings, including “walk or “manner.” Since there are similarities and equivalencies in more than one of the possible meanings of each of these two words, the Greek is obviously a translation of The Hebrew word HaHalakha.

lust and delusion, * *23 to be reformed in your spirits and your*
minds, 24 and put on * *the new person, the one created*
according to Elohim, in the righteousness and the holiness of
the truth. *

25 Therefore, lay aside falsehood, each of you speak the
truth with his neighbor, because we are parts of the same
body. 26 Be angry, but don't sin; don't let the sun set on your

---

* 4:22 — Here we see the counterpoint to the factual nature of the Bible: the deluded nature of Paganism. Since the Bible is absolute truth, anything which denies it is falsehood and delusion.

* 4:24a — The Greek word used here for "put on" typically refers to clothing oneself. This is a connection of the Biblical Commandment of the Mikveh, the Immersion. In the Torah, the wording typically used literally translates as "to immerse one's garments." The idea of this wording is that after the ritual of purification one must step into a clean and pure life. After all, a person does not take a bath and then put on filthy clothes. Thus the ritual of purification is null and void if the person steps right back into the filth of their sins. So the people who converted from paganism must leave all their former paganism behind and live a new life in the biblical lifestyle.

* 4:24b — The Torah is referred to in Judaism as "the Torah of Truth." The righteousness and Holiness of the Truth is a lifestyle that upholds God's 613 Commandments found in the Torah. All of the Commandments in the Bible, whether a Jewish Tanakh or a Christian Bible, are found in the first

five books, the Torah. Outside of the Torah we have "commands," which are orders that God gives that are limited to specific conditions, times, and specific individuals. These commands are not eternal and are not part of the Law. There are also explanations of Commandments found outside the Torah, as we see in the Teachings of Yshu`a recorded in the four Bsorat (Gospels).

It should be noted that most people who object to the idea of obeying the Commandments either do not know them at all, or know some but do not understand them. Some of the Commandments are unclear when translated out of the Original Hebrew, and some require a background base of knowledge that most Twenty First Century people lack. This knowledge is recorded in various Rabbinical works, but most Christians would never think to read "another religion's" books to understand their own Bible. This is understandable due to the centuries that have passed since the time when followers were all part of a distinctly Jewish expression of their faith in God and in Messiah.

Fortunately, Christianity has preserved the Jewish knowledge that Yshu`a is the Messiah, and Orthodox Judaism has preserved most of how He taught His followers to live. The Bsorat preserves the teachings of Yshu`a. What we need to understand is that He addressed very traditional Jews. We must start with First Century Pharisaic Judaism: If He did not address a particular element of that religion, that element is acceptable by God.

anger,[*] 27 *nor give an opportunity the Traducer*[*].
28 *Do not let the thief steal any longer; instead, command
him to labor well by hand, so that he will have something to
give those in need.*[*]
29 *Do not allow any condemning, worthless words come
from your mouth, but only any good [words] to edify those in*

---

[*] 4:26 — The first part of this verse is believed to be a quote of Psalm 4:5 (4:4 in the Christian Bible). The Hebrew of Psalm 4:5 uses "רִגְזוּ (rigzu)," which translates as "tremble," but in the Greek text this is translated as "οργιζεσθε. (orgizesthe)" which means, "to become angry." This may have been meant to remind the reader of Psalm 4:5 suggesting that our awe of God will help us to prevent anger from developing into sin.

This verse refutes the idea that anger is intrinsically bad. It makes it very clear that it is harboring anger, and letting it become resentment and hatred that is sinful. Situations that cause anger must be resolved quickly to prevent resentment and hatred. This is not always easy because we desire to make peace, but sometimes we settle for the easy false peace of silence rather than resolving issues.

[*] 4:27 — The Greek word used here is "Διαβολω (Diabolo), " which we usually translate as "devil." However, the literal meaning is very important to the meaning of the verse. "Diabolo" literally means "someone who shames or accuses others by using falsehood or misrepresentation." This is a more complete description of HaSatan than "Devil" or even "the

Accuser." It indicates HaSatan's use of falsehood to bring people to ruin. Certainly, if all humanity were fully aware of God and Messiah, and fully knowledgeable of the Torah, and fully aware of the nature of sin and all the pain that sin causes both themselves and other people, all humanity would choose to be Torah observant. Unfortunately, mankind is not that aware of reality. People have made up false "gods." People have denounced the existence of God. As a result, confusion and doubt corrupt humanity.

This word also indicates that we should avoid situations that would invite false accusations. When people become angered and do not communicate about that anger, it is possible that the angry person is being angry without cause. If he was open with the person who offended him, that person might well apologize and make amends if applicable. It is also possible that the offense was a simple misunderstanding that is easily rectified by a few simple words.

* 4:28 — The Torah commands a repentant thief to return what was stolen plus one fifth of its value. Obviously, Shaul's advice here is in addition to obeying the Torah. This advise would remove from the thief the temptation to steal since he would now earn an honest wage and the addition of having him provide charity for those in need would help to establish in him the exact opposite way of thinking. Bad habits are best overcome by replacing them with good habits.

need that may stir up chesed to those hearing. * [30] *And do not grieve the Ruach Elohim HaKadosh,* * *by whom you were attested for a judgment of redemption.* * [31] *Extinguish in you all bitterness, and rage, and vengeance, and outcry, and Lashon HaRa with all evil things.* * [32] *And, be kind sympathetic, and forgiving to each other yourselves, as*

---

* 4:29 — Rabbi Shaul uses the Hebrew concept of Lashon HaRa (the Evil Tongue) here rather than the typical definition of gossip or slander. It does not matter if the words are true or not; their hurtful nature makes them Lashon HaRa. The Jewish concept of Lashon HaRa is very much in keeping with the teachings of Yshu`a.

Yshu`a taught on the concept of Kavanah (intention) many times in the Bible. Specifically, obeying God with our actions is not enough if our motivations are impure. Lashon HaRa is defined by the hurtful intentions of the words, not their veracity. Even the same sentence can be either good or bad depending on the motivations of the speaker. The question is: "Does the speaker seek to help a person or hurt a person?" If their motivation is to help a person avoid sin, they may say that another person is a seducer (a person who leads others into sin), but they cannot say those same words simply because they dislike the other person even if the words are true.

* 4:30a — The Greek used here is "Πνευμα το Αγιον του Θεου (Pneuma to Agion tou Theos)," which means, "The Holy Spirit [of] the God." The use of the definite article modifying

Theos (God) is a derivative of Hebrew grammar and sets the Real God apart from mythical "gods." The Greek word "Θεου (Theos)" best translates as the Hebrew Name for God, "Elohim." This is the only place where this term is used. This phrase also links the Bsorat (Gospel) phrase "Πνευμα Αγιον (Pneuma Agios, Holy Spirit)" with the Hebrew phrase "אלהים רוח (Ruach Elohim, Spirit of God)."

* 4:30b — The second half of this verse must be translated by considering all possible meanings of the Greek words. The direct literal meaning makes little sense and could be interpreted to disagree with other of Rabbi Shaul's writings. The Greek word "ημεραν (hemeran)" literally means the time in between night and day. Figuratively, it's meanings range from day, year, age, and judgment. Based on overall context, "judgment" is the correct way to translate the word in this sentence.

This passage when translated in this manner agrees with the rest of Shaul's writings and the Bible. The popular translation, "…by whom you were sealed for a day of redemption" disagrees with Hebrews 10:26-29 (which was presumably written by Rabbi Shaul himself) where the author asserts that only saved believers can commit the unforgivable sin of "blasphemy against the Holy Spirit." It also disagrees with the prophecies of the Day of Judgment by not using the definite article, which would signify a single day of judgment.

* 4:31 — Here the rabbi lists the most common sins that can result from harboring anger and hurt.

*Elohim, in Messiah, forgave you.**

5 [1] *Therefore be imitators of Elohim, as beloved children;**
[2] *and walk in love, just as Messiah loved us, and surrendered*
himself for us, as an offering, and a sacrifice to Elohim with a
pleasing aroma. [3] *But as is fitting the Sanctified People, do*
not allow sexual sins and all uncleanness and greediness to be
*named among you,** [4] *and filthiness and speaking stupidly or*

---

* 4:32 — Here the rabbi gives a list of the actions that cure the problems caused by harboring anger and hurt. Obviously a quick resolution of the situation is important whenever possible.

* 5:1 — A basic tenant of Judaism is that HaShem never sins. This means that HaShem is not a hypocrite when he gives us Commandments. Also, the idea of the child emulating the parent is universal. So, Rabbi Shaul portrays Torah observance as a natural part of being saved. This does not mean that Torah observance is a condition of salvation, but rather as the natural path that a Believer takes upon receiving salvation.

* 5:3 — Some people have assumed that this verse means that these topics cannot be discussed. There are actually two meanings for this verse. In the simplest sense, it means that we cannot put ourselves in situations where immoral behavior would be assumed to have occurred. The Believer should live a life that does not even invite false accusations of immoral behavior.

Interpreting the verse on the Sod level of interpretation brings a second meaning to the verse. The use of the Greek word "ονομαζεσθω (onomazestho)," referring to naming something is significant. To name something is to give it identity and therefore importance and even power. Thus to speak of these sins as if they were in any way acceptable lifestyle choices is wrong and promotes evil. (For more on Sod, see Appendix 4.)

For example: a few years ago people made up terms to use to refer to a person with whom another person regularly commits sexual sins of a homosexual nature. Now, not even two decades latter, people are insisting on redefining the word "marriage" to include homosexual pairings. The Rabbinical interpretation of the Commandment "לֹא תִנְאָף (Lo tinaf – the prohibition against adultery)" does not simply cover sexual sins but also any action that betrays the covenant of marriage or mocks the institution of marriage. Therefore even pretending that two people of the same gender can become married is a sin. So even naming that sin "a marriage" is in and of itself a sin.

LINGUISTIC NOTE: The Greek idea of betrayal in a marriage was purely sexual. So, the Greek word had a distinctly sexual definition. The Biblical definition of marriage contained more responsibilities, and the Biblical prohibition against betrayal in marriage goes beyond the sexual. So, our English translations which use Greek translations as references give us a more Greek definition that a Biblical one.

joking*; but rather thanksgiving*. 5 For know this: everyone
that is a sexual sinner, or unclean or a greedy person who is
an idol-worshiper, has inheritance in the Kingdom of the
Messiah and Elohim.* 6 Let no one deceive you with empty
words; for through these comes the punishment of Elohim
upon the Sons of Rebellion. 7 Therefore do not be their co-
participants.*
*8 For you were then darkness; but now, light through

---

* 5:4a — The use of "η (ey)," which means "or," rather than "και (kai)," which means "and," between "speaking stupidly" and "joking" indicates that the same item in the list is being renamed. As such the "stupidly" applies to both. Thus we see that joking is not forbidden in and of itself.

  Using the same literary techniques in which Rabbi Shaul was trained, we use the proceeding and following verses to determine the context in which the word "stupidly" applies in this verse. Both verse three and verse four condemns the same three groups of sins: sexual sins, uncleanness, and greed. So, it is easy to see that any humor or speech that seeks to make these three groups of sins socially acceptable is defined by this passage as "stupid" and is forbidden.

* 5:4b — When a person is truly grateful for all that God and Messiah have done for mankind as well as for each of us as individuals, that person wants to express his or her gratitude in a meaningful way. The best way to do this is to obey God's Commandments as Messiah instructed us to do.

* 5:5 — This verse must be understood in its entirety. Greedy, sexually immoral or impure people are not forgiven if their immorality becomes idolatrous. This to say that they place such a high importance on their sinful pursuits that these pursuits become more important than God to them. A follower of Messiah may not be perfect; he or she may make a mistake from time to time, but a follower of Messiah strives to serve God, values his or her relationship with God, and regrets any sins he or she may have committed in a moment of weakness.

* 5:6&7 — Many people make excuses for immoral behavior. Some people even use the promise of salvation as an excuse to commit evil actions. This is "blasphemy against the Holy Spirit," as defined in the Bible (Hebrews 10 26-29). Of course, the definition in Hebrews 10:26-29 is an addition to the definition given in Numbers 15:30-31. Therefore, all conditions of both verses must apply. Repentance after the action, but before one is brought to judgment negates the remorseless arrogance implied by the Hebrew of our passage in the Book of Numbers. (See Appendix Six for a more complete discussion of blasphemy against the Holy Spirit.)

* 5:8-10 — The word "light" is frequently used metaphorically as "Torah." Verse 9 restates the fact that the Torah defines what constitutes goodness, righteousness, and truth. Verse 10 continues with a more direct mention of determining what pleases HaShem. Specifically, The Bible defines exactly what actions are moral and what actions are immoral. We human beings do not have that authority.

Adonai; walk as children of light. [9] *For the fruit of the light is in all goodness, righteousness and truth,* [10] *proving what is fully agreeable to Adonai.* [11] *And do not share company with the unfruitful works of darkness, but rather reprove [them],** [12] *for it is shameful to even speak of the hidden things they do.*
[13] *But all things that are reproved are revealed by the light*,*
[14] *This is why it says,*

"Arise, sleeping one!
Stand up from the dead,
and Messiah will shine on you!" *

[15] *Therefore, watch carefully how you walk* — not as the unwise, but as the wise.* [16] *Improve the opportunity of the time, because the age is evil.** [17] *Because of this, do not be*

---

* 5:11 — Here "darkness" has two meanings. The first is ignorance, specifically ignorance of Torah. The second is Antinomianism, rejection of Torah. Antinomianism is a far more sinister darkness. Those who seek to follow Messiah cannot associate with those who reject Messiah's command to obey the entire Torah. Also we should be mindful of the meaning of the word "reprove." "Reprove" is used here to indicate the contrast between the actions of the Follower of Messiah and the evil doer. It does not mean to condemn the person who walks in spiritual darkness, but rather to be a good example by doing positive, good actions.

* 5:13 — Throughout the ages there have been men arrogant enough to think that they have the right to define what is good and what is evil, but these things were determined by God before He created the

world. The World itself is created based upon His definition, which the Torah, God's light, sets down as Commandments. This verse acknowledges that only the Word of God has the authority to establish these definitions.

* 5:14 — The portion quoted here is a series of verse fragments. Shaul first quotes part of Isaiah 60:1, then part of Isaiah 26:19, and concludes with part of Isaiah 60:2 with "Messiah" being substituted for "the Glory of HaShem." The substitution is correct because of the Unity of Elohim (the Father, the Son, and the Holy Spirit). Furthermore, the passages all refer to Messiah's return. Rabbi Shaul is using a mnemonic technique frequent in Judaism to allude to a connection between the two passages. One passage refers to the glory of God being revealed, the next refers to the resurrection of the dead. Yshu`a HaMashiach accomplishes both.

* 5:15 — The Hebrew word for walk, Halakha, is also the word used for how we apply the Commandments to our lives. Rabbi Shaul is obviously using the spiritual definition here.

* 5:16 — In eras when evil abounds it is necessary to ensure that one's time is not wasted in sinful pursuits. In times of less evil, good behavior comes more naturally and less effort is required to overcome temptation.

*stupid, but understand what the will of Adonai is.**
18 * *And do not get drunk in wine in which there is*
complete debauchery, but be filled with the Spirit —*
19 *speaking to yourselves in Psalms, religious odes, and*
spiritual cantillation, singing and playing music in your
heart to Adonai;* 20 *always give thanks for everything to God*
the Father in the name of our Lord Yshuà the Messiah.
*21 *Submit to each other in awe of the Messiah.* 22 *Wives*
submit to your husbands as to Adonai, 23 *because the man is*
head of the wife, as also Messiah, is head of the [Messianic]
Rabbinate, and He is savior to the body. 24 *But as the*
[Messianic] Rabbinate is submitted to Messiah, so also are the
*wives to their husbands in everything.**

---

* 5:17 — Again Rabbi Shaul pleads with the people to seek knowledge of what HaShem wants from us. His strong wording may not be politically correct, but it is an honest appraisal of the condition of a person who chooses not to seek knowledge of God's will for us.

* 5:18-20 — Rabbi Shaul gives instruction on things to do. As a wise teacher, Rabbi Shaul does not make prohibitions without obligations. That means that he does not take away without giving. He asks the people to give up evil actions and then gives them alternative good actions.

* 5:18 — The clarifying phrase "in which there is complete debauchery" specifies that the moderation taught by Yshu`a and Judaism as a whole is not abrogated here. It is not a sin to drink wine in moderation, but it is a

sin to drink enough to impair your ability to resist temptation.

* 5:19 — This passage refers to specific worship practices of Judaism. "Speaking to yourselves in Psalms" refers to reading the Book of Psalms; "religious odes" refers to any theologically correct religious song or poem not found in the Bible; "spiritual cantillation" refers to the traditional melodies used in singing the Torah and the Prayers during synagogue service. The Greek translated as "cantillation" is "ωδαις (odais)," which specifically refers to the cantillation in a Jewish synagogue service.

* 5:21-6:9 — Rabbi Shaul outlines proper interpersonal relationships. He gives guidelines as to how we should relate to each other. He has already covered the general concept of not harboring resentment. Now, he outlines specific guidelines for various relationships.

* 5:21-24 — The Commandment that wives should submit to their husbands has been the target of much anti-biblical rhetoric. These attacks on God's plan for marriage only seem to have validity when the husbands fail to obey HaShem's plan for their role in marriage. When the husband properly executes his role in marriage, the wife's role is not a burden for a godly woman. Conversely, when the wife refuses her biblical role in marriage, the husband becomes resentful, to a degree. This degree may be unconscious, but it is present and effects his attitude towards her. (Note: see comment on Ephesians 5:25-33 for comparison.)

*25 * The husbands, love the wives, just as the Messiah loved the [Messianic] Community and surrendered Himself up on its behalf, 26 so that he could sanctify it, cleansing the Mikveh, as per the Oral Word,* 27 that it could present to Him in glory the [Messianic] Community having no defilement or wrinkle or any such thing, but that it be holy and unblemished.* 28 In this way husbands are obligated: to love their wives as much as they love their own bodies; he that loves his wife is loving himself. 29 Because, no one ever hates his own flesh; he nourishes it and cherishes it, just as the Messiah [does] the [Messianic] Community, 30 because we are members of His body. 31 "Therefore, a man will leave his father and mother*

---

* 5:25-33 — The husband's role in Marriage is spelled out very clearly. He has two primary obligations to his wife. These are given in order of importance. First, he is required to ensure her spiritual correctness. This entails both her salvation and her righteousness in accordance with the Torah. Second, he must cherish her placing her wellbeing before his own. If the husband fulfills both of these obligations, the wife will not feel oppressed in her godly submission to her husband. (Note: see comment on Ephesians 5:21-24 for comparison.)

* 5:26 — This verse is extremely significant to the Followers of Messiah. The Biblical Commandments concerning Immersion were already part of Judaism for about 1500 years at this time of Messiah. It is easy for us to see looking back that Messiah was the operating force in the Mikveh Immersion from the beginning. However, Rabbi Shaul asserts this so that

there is no doubt: the spiritual cleansing of the Immersion derives its power from Messiah.

Furthermore, Rabbi Shaul says that because Yshu`a followed the Oral Law concerning the Mikveh, the traditional procedure found in the Oral Law is now the method that is ordained by Yshu`a. So, while many Christians may dispute the validity of the Talmud, also known as the Oral Law, Rabbi Shaul asserts that Yshu`a ordained the method which is recorded in the Talmud.

Following the Traditional technique used for thousands of years would seem logical to a traditional Jew who accepts Yshu`a as Messiah. One might say that this is an aesthetic option. After all many Christians who visit Israel become immersed in the Jordan River in a kosher manner for aesthetic reasons. However, this verse makes the traditional procedure the commanded procedure. The symbolism of each aspect of the Mikveh is inspiring and informative, teaching us about Messiah.

* 5:27 — The Greek wording here simply does not translate into an easy to understand grammatically correct sentence. While it states that the Mikveh presents us to Him in glory, it also indicates that He, Himself is the operating force by which this happens.

and cling to his wife, and the two will become one flesh."* [32]
This is great mystery, but I speak concerning Messiah and the
[Messianic] Community, [33] *but also, concerning you, each*
and everyone: love his wife as himself, and wife revere the
husband.

6 [1] *Children, obey your parents, for this is right in*
Adonai. [2] *"Honor your father and mother" which is the first*
Commandment with a promise [3] *"that it may be well with*
you, and that you may be long lived in the Land."
[4] *Fathers, do not provoke your children but make them,*
but nurture them in education and the Torah *of Adonai.**
*[5] *Slaves, obey your physical masters with fear, and*
trembling in sincerity of your heart as to Messiah, [6] *not after*

---

* 5:31 — This quote from Genesis 2:24 is placed here to remind us that this is not a new thing. This plan for a happy marriage has always been part of God's plan for us. It also tells us what modern science is currently discovering: that men and women each have different mental and emotional strengths. By quoting Genesis 2:24, Rabbi Shaul is telling us that God intentionally created us this way. So, each person of either gender is designed to fulfill his or her role in a marriage. Forcing ourselves into roles for which we were not designed causes us stress and unhappiness.

* 6:4 — The Greek word used here is "νουθεσια (nouthesia)," which means "instruction." This is the literal meaning of the Hebrew word "Torah." The term "Torah of Adonai" is a very specific reference

to the Torah, the first five books of the Bible, in which all of the Commandments are found. Culturally this also makes sense because a father is responsible to teach the Torah to his children prior to their Bar/Bat Mitzvah. While the Bat Mitzvah is a newer ceremony, the girls were still taught how to live godly lives.

* 6:1-4 — Here again both parties are given responsibilities. Children must obey their parents, and parents must act like proper, godly parents and encourage the child to obey them by being reasonable with their children. Parents teach their children more than they realize. Parents who do not live proper, godly lives accidentally teach ungodliness to their children.

* 6:5-9 — Again with respect to masters and slaves, Rabbi Shaul spells out responsibilities for both parties. It should be understood that the slavery spoken of in the Bible was a far more humane system that that which was instituted by non-Jews throughout human history. Slaves were fed, clothed, and housed at least as well as their masters. Slaves had rights specifically spelled out in the Torah.

It is probably because the Torah places so many burdens upon the master that Rabbi Shaul addresses most of his comments in this passage to the obligations of the slave. By this time in Jewish history, the rabbis, scribes and priests had studied the Torah and established many chumrot, strictures designed to help prevent inadvertent violation of the Mitzvot regarding the responsibilities of the master.

the manner of sight-labor, as sycophants,* but as servants of*
Messiah, doing Elohim's will from [your] soul, 7 serving with
kindness as to Adonai and not men, 8 knowing that
whomsoever does this will get benefit from Adonai, whether
slave of freeman.
9 And masters, treat your slaves the same way. Don't
threaten them. Remember that in heaven both you and they
have the same Master, and he has no favorites.
**10 In conclusion, my brothers, be strengthened in Adonai,*

---

* 6:6a — The Greek word “οφθαλμοδουλιαν (ophthalmodoulian)” does not translate directly into English nor does it translate culturally. “Sight-labor” is the best approximation. It refers to unskilled laborers who are known to be lazy, and due to their lack of marketable skills are relegated to the most laborious manual labor. Because of the untrustworthiness of these workers, an overseer had to keep them in his sight at all times to ensure their continued work.

* 6:6b — The Greek word “ανθρωπαρεσκοι (anthropareskoi),” is a combination of two words, literally translating as “man-pleaser.” It refers to a fawning, unscrupulous person who will do anything to curry the favor of those he sees as his superiors. The English word “sycophant” conveys this meaning more completely than breaking down the Greek word into its component parts and rendering a hyphenate as the translation.

* 6:10-18 — Rabbi Shaul discusses our spirituality in martial terms. The metaphor of the “Armor of God”

may well be inspired by his own beleaguered circumstances. He sees himself not as a political criminal despite the fact that Rome's basis for calling Rabbi Shaul a criminal was purely political. The Messianic movement was by the Romans seen as "destabilizing" to the Empire. However, Rabbi Shaul obviously sees himself as a "prisoner of war" in the spiritual war between God and all evil.

Rabbi Shaul was well aware of something that we who live in a multi-cultural environment seem to forget all too easily. This is that spiritually there are only two positions that a person may take: Good (siding with and obeying God) and evil (everything else). Many of us are so afraid to sound like bigots that they fail to stand up for righteousness.

We should be willing to admit that we are obliged to uphold God's Commandments despite the fact that we are saved by God's Chesed. More importantly, we need to be willing to stand up for righteousness within the body of Messiah. Yshu`a said that we must remove the log from our eye before attempting to remove the speck from someone else's eye. Too many believers in Messiah are willing to attack oppress or offend people who have not yet accepted Yshu`a as Messiah, but refuse to actually follow Yshu`a's teachings. Many congregational leaders are too worried that teaching what Yshu`a taught would drive people out of the congregation; they become too concerned with the institution of their congregation and they disregard the purpose of the congregation. Sin is evil. We should have the courage to say this.

and in the power of His strength![*] [11] *Put on the full armor*[*] *of Elohim, to be able to stand against the trickery of the Traducer.* [12] *because we are not wrestling against flesh and blood, but against the principalities, and powers and against This World's rulers of darkness, against the spiritual evil in the high places.*[*] [13] *Because of this, take up the full armor of Elohim; so that you will be able to resist in the day of evil, and stand, having accomplished absolutely all.*[*] [14] *Therefore, stand, having girded your waist with truth,*[*] *and putting*

---

[*] 6:11 — Th Greek text uses the word "πανοπλιαν (panoplian)." This is a name for a specific type of armor. Panoplian was the most protective armor that the Greeks used. It was frequently reserved for officers or elite soldiers and officers only. Symbolically both aspects of this definition are meaningful to this verse. First, the Armor of Elohim is the most protective that there is because only the protection that God devised for us can totally protect us from evil. Second, God gave His armor to the Jews, who could be seen as His elite soldiers in the war between good and evil, and they have distributed this armor to the rest of the body of believers; so that now, the difference between the "elite" and the common is not a matter of bloodline, but of how much of this "officer's uniform of faith" each individual chooses to put on.

[*] 6:12 — Obviously, Rabbi Shaul sees himself as victorious in this spiritual warfare. Despite his physical imprisonment, he sees his circumstances, and those of all others who stand up for what is right, as part of

a spiritual battle. This shows the interconnected nature of the spiritual and the physical worlds. One cannot fight the spiritual battle without taking physical actions. You cannot be on God's side spiritually, if you work against Him in the physical sense.

* 6:13 — Since our real battle is spiritual, earthly sufferings do not effect our spiritual victory. Only by giving in to evil can we loose the spiritual war. The phrase "...having accomplished all," is very important. We know from the narrative that we are discussing resisting temptation, and we know that God does forgive sins. So, the word "all" does not mean "all six hundred and thirteen Mitzvot," and it does not mean "which ever Mitzvot we choose to obey." It can only mean that we have accomplished all that we are capable of accomplishing. This means that we must put out our genuine best effort for God. It is easy for us to excuse our own shortcomings and say that we are doing our best when we are not really trying. We must be honest with ourselves, evaluate our lives and seek to improve those areas that can be improved. In order to be the best that we can be, we must strive to uphold all 613 Mitzvot. Then, if we are unable to uphold all 613, we truly know that we honestly have accomplished our best.

stand, having girded your waist with truth, and putting on the put on breastplate of righteousness,* 15 and having shod your feet with the preparation of the Bsorat of peace.* 16*
Above all having taken up the shield of moral conviction, by which you will be able to quench all the arrows that the Evil

---

* 6:14a — The term "having girded your waist with truth" draws metaphorically from the girdle, which was used to prevent a soldier from injuring himself. The girdle was a very wide belt that prevented damage to the kidneys. This damage could occur without even a battle, due to the jarring of riding a horse and the strain of carrying heavy weapons and wearing armor. Basically the Girdle prevented self-inflicted injuries. Today weightlifters wear a similar device, which is usually called a "kidney belt" to prevent them from hurting themselves.

The word "Truth" is meant in two simultaneous ways. First, in the simplistic meaning it refers to the fact that our faith is based entirely on truth. Second, it refers to the Blessing of the Torah, which calls the Torah "the Torah of Truth." So this Girdle of Truth is Torah study, because by failing to study the Word of God we injure ourselves. Living a biblical, Torah observant lifestyle protects us from many evil influences, while sin leaves us vulnerable to HaSatan, giving him a degree of power over our lives.

* 6:14b — The term "Breastplate of Righteousness" follows a similar metaphorical model. The Breastplate is part of a soldier's armor. Righteousness is something

that you can and must do for yourself. This is not the same as Salvation and is not to be confused with the fact that God treats those who are saved as if they were righteous. This means that living according to Torah actually protects us from HaSatan.

The intent behind all the Commandments of the Torah is to bring us closer to HaShem. The Commandments still have that effect when we live them out of love for HaShem and without the corrupting influence of legalism (the attempt to misuse the Commandments as a means of salvation).

* 6:15 — The wording of this verse seems to deviate slightly from the rest in that the effect of the metaphorical shoes is spelled out with the word "preparation," instead of a word for shoes being used. This deviation is made by Rabbi Shaul to ensure that even the non-Jews who read the letter see that he is referencing the Book of Exodus. When about to depart from Egypt, on the night of the Passover, the Jews were commanded to eat the Passover while prepared to leave the evil place forever, with their shoes on their feet.

The rabbi is clearly focusing his thought on the fact that the ultimate death, damnation, passes over the followers of Messiah. To this is added the Halakha, "the Walk" or "the Way," which is how we apply Torah to our lives. In this case Rabbi Shaul specifically refers to the manner in which Messiah taught us to apply the Torah to our lives.

One ignites.[*] [17]*And take the helmet of Salvation,*[*] *and the*

---

[*] 6:16 — The Term "Shield of Faith" returns us to the format that the Rabbi has already established. Here, as opposed to the Breastplate mentioned in 6:14b, we have a shield — a protection that is not part of our armor. This shield represents Salvation though Messiah, because you cannot save yourself, you must rely on Yshu`a. Also, the shield is described as protecting the believers from HaSatan's fire. No other part of this spiritual armor is described as directly overcoming HaSatan. The shield was also marked with an identifying symbol, writing or icon. This also indicates that we must identify ourselves with the Messiah.

It is worthy to note that "πιστεως (pisteos)," the Greek word usually translated as "faith" has the same meaning as the Hebrew word Emmunah, both of which are different from our English word "faith." While "faith" refers to a belief without the need for proof, "emmunah" and "pisteos" both mean "moral conviction," which is to say a moral belief that is strong enough to effect the person's decision making processes. So, the "faith" discussed in the Bible is not a faith without actions; it is a faith that inspires actions.

This verse says that we will be able to quench the flames that the Evil One ignites. This is true. Unfortunately, many people do not realize that not all temptation comes from HaSatan. Most of the Temptations we must overcome originate from other people who have been corrupted to the point that

HaSatan does not need to tempt them further. Of course, there is little difference between this outside temptation and the one authored by HaSatan himself.

A good deal of other temptation come upon us from within. Many people lead themselves into temptation. God will give us the strength to overcome outside temptation, but our internal temptations are part of our freedom of choice. God will help us to become better people, but we must admit that these temptations come from ourselves before we are ready to accept His help.

Very much like a drug addict, many people are addicted to sin and evil. They re-name the evil to make it more acceptable and less embarrassing just as discussed in Ephesians 5:1-17. People use terms like "out of order,' "not right [with God]," "not Torah observant," rather than admitting that any violation of any Commandment is a sin, and sin is evil.

* 6:17a — The "Helmet of Salvation" brings to mind the helmets of the era, which were indicators of rank and of allegiance. It is a simple matter to understand that a person who has been delivered from evil is of a higher status than a person who has not been delivered. Messiah came to deliver us from evil, not simply to save us from the punishment that we, as sinners deserve.

Our deliverance takes the form of Messiah's teachings on how we may avoid sin and the indwelling of the Holy Spirit, which gives us the ability to make better, more godly, choices as well as our opportunity to accept Yshu`a as our Messiah for salvation in the World to come. Since we make these choices with our minds, the helmet is the piece of armor chosen to represent this working of the man with the support of the Holy Spirit and the knowledge of Messiah.

The Greek word used here is, "σωτηριου (soteriou)." This is the same word used in the Septuagint to translate the Hebrew word "יְשׁוּעָה (Yshu`ah)." Yshu`ah is the common word for Salvation and the word from which the name "יְשׁוּעַ (Yshu`a)" is derived.

Note on Salvation:
Since the text here refers to salvation, and since there are differing opinions about salvation, I would like to pause here to clarify my understanding of Salvation so that I am not misunderstood. I do not support works-based salvation theories or "easy-sleazy-grace" theories of salvation. As usual, God's plan is balanced between extremes.

In English, there appears to be a paradox in the Bible. We read that Salvation comes from faith, but Yshu`a also says that those who work against the Law are damned (Matthew 7:21-23). Then we read that the author of Hebrews (usually believed to be Rabbi Shaul) states that the refusal to accept any one of the 613 Commandments is blasphemy against the Holy Spirit.

We know that truth does not disagree with truth and that the Bible is true. So now we must ask "How do these passages agree with each other?"

The first thing to do is remember that we need to go back to the original language(s). While most of the existing ancient texts of the Messianic Scriptures are written in Greek, Yshu`a spoke Hebrew. So it is helpful to know how Hebrew was translated into Greek in the First Century CE.

The Hebrew texts use the word "emmunah" and the Greek texts use the word "pisteos." These have about the same meaning: a moral conviction that is strong enough to effect our decision making process. This conviction by definition must be strong enough to inspire us to do works. The Hebrew and Greek texts both agree that salvation is based upon a moral conviction. So then, works do not earn salvation but the same mental/spiritual quality that causes us to be saved also causes us to do good works as defined by the 613 Commandments. The one cause has two effects, one observable in this world, the other not observable in this world.

See Appendix Six for a discussion of Blasphemy against the Holy Spirit and the possibility of Loss of salvation.

sword given by the Spirit, which is the Word of Elohim; * 18
Through all, pray and petition, praying all the time, in the
Spirit, and for the same thing guarding without fail and
petitioning for all the Sanctified People, * 19 *and me, that I*
may be given speech when I open my mouth, in boldness to
make known the mystery of the Bsorat, 20 *for the sake of*
which, I am an ambassador in chains that in it I may speak
boldly, in the manner that it is necessary for me to speak. *

---

* 6:17b — We finally get to our one weapon, "The Sword given by the Spirit, that is the Word of God." To overcome obstacles and enemies that would bar our way to heaven, we must have a weapon. Our weapon is the Word of God, the Torah. The Scriptures contain either direct instructions or examples of how we should deal with almost every situation. The lessons learned from these scriptures also give us the insight and wisdom to deal with any other situations in a godly manner. Additionally, the Bsorat Yochanan, John, 1:1-5 describes Yshu`a as the Word — He is the living Torah. Therefore we should also draw from His example of how the Torah is applied to our lives.

* 6:18 — This verse is a transition between verse seventeen and nineteen. As such, using the theme of juxtaposition that we see in the Torah, it links Prayer with both Deliverance and the Scriptures. This is because Messiah promised to grant all prayers ask for in His name. This term, "in His name," loses meaning in English. It does not simply mean to pronounce the phonetics of Messiah's name in order

to have any prayer granted; it means to pray in Messiah's identity. This means in Yshu`a's character and by His authority.

Since it is against Messiah's character to violate any Commandment, you cannot pray in His name for the ability to violate a Commandment. Furthermore, since the biblical examples show us that evil must be conquered without us committing any sins, we must rely upon the Word of God to teach us how we may pray, what we may ask and what we may not ask.

* 6:19&20 — Rabbi Shaul asks to be prayed for that he may have the courage to tell the truth about Yshu`a and proclaim Yshu`a as Messiah even in the face of the torture and possible execution that he expected from the Romans.

Two purposes are served by this public call for prayer…

One: The entire Messianic Community would see that the opposition that Rabbi Shaul faced in spreading the word of Messiah was not just political, as the Romans saw it. It truly was part of a struggle between good and evil, and the entire Messianic Community was/is part of that struggle.

Two: By having all the followers of Messiah pray for him, Rabbi Shaul is demonstrating that his courage comes from the Lord, not from himself. This was undoubtedly intended much as many of Moshe's actions, to deflect praise from the man and direct it to God, to Whom all praise is due.

*21 So that you may now, also know the things about me —
what I am doing, Tychicus,* the beloved brother and a
trustworthy shamash in Adonai, will make all things known
to you. 22 Whom I sent to you, for this same thing, so that
you may know the things about us, and invoke comfort in
your heart.**

*23 Peace to the brothers, and love with moral conviction in
Elohim Abba and Adonai Yshuà HaMashiach. 24 Chesed with
all those loving Adoneynu Yshuà HaMashiach in
immortality.**

---

* 6:21 — Tychicus: an assistant of Rabbi Shaul mentioned also in Titus 3:12. He apparently acted as a Messenger when needed, and delivered the autograph of this letter to whomever it was originally sent.

* 6:22 — Rabbi Shaul does not tell all of his problems in this letter because it is his intention to have Tychicus relate the situation to the people gently, so as not to cause any more alarm to the people than is unavoidable.

* 6:24 — Rabbi Shaul closes by wishing God's grace on those who love Him. Then he clarifies that this love must be undying. While he is not demanding that all followers of Messiah become martyrs, he is obliquely stating that this love must be strong enough to encourage the person to serve God in the face of adversity. This brings to mind Rabbi Ya`akov Ben Yosef's (James') assertion that "Faith without works is dead" (The letter of Rabbi Ya`akov ben Yosef (James) 2:17).

EPHESIANS

without commentary

EPHESIANS

1 1 [From:] Sha'ul, by Elohim's decree, a representative of
the Messiah Yshuà
To: Sanctified People being on ________ [in Ephesus],
and having moral conviction in, the Messiah, Yshuà, 2 Chesed
to you and peace from Elohim, our Father and the Adonai
Yshuà, the Messiah.

3 Praised be Elohim, Father of Adoneynu Yshuà, the
Messiah, who has blessed us with every spiritual blessing in
Heaven through Messiah. 4 Just as he chose us before the
creation of the universe to exist holy and sinless before Him in
love. 5 He established before the beginning that by the actions
of Yshuà the Messiah we would be adopted as His sons —
according to the satisfaction of His desire — 6 So to the praise
of the manifest glory of His chesed, with which He favored us
in love.

7 In whom, we have redemption because of His blood —
the pardon of mistakes by means of the abundance of His
chesed, 8 which abounds for us in all wisdom and intelligence.
9 He has revealed to us the secret of what He desires according
to His kindness which He exhibited in Himself. 10 for the
stewardship of the fullness of the proper time — to bring
together as one everything, in Messiah – the things in Heaven
and the things on earth.

11 In Whom also we were allotted the inheritance,
previously chosen according to setting forth all things to work
according to the volition of His will, 12 for those of us having
previously trusted in Messiah to be a praise to His glory.

13 In Whom also, you, having heard the word of truth, the good news of the salvation of your [souls], in Whom, also believing, you were sealed with the promise of the Ruach HaKodesh, 14 Who is a guarantee of our inheritance until the redemption of salvation, [for you] to be a praise to His glory.

15 Therefore, hearing of the moral conviction among you in Adonai, Yshuà, and the love for the righteous people, 16 I have not ceased giving thanks on your behalf, making mention in my prayers, 17 may Elohim, Adoneynu, Yshuà HaMashiach, Father of Glory, give to you a spirit of wisdom and revelation of knowledge of Him, 18 having illuminated the eyes of your mind that you may know what the hope of His calling is, and what the riches of the glory of His inheritance among the sanctified are, 19 and what the surpassing greatness of his power working in us who believe according to the power of His strength, 20 which He worked in the Messiah raising Him from the dead, and seating Him at His right hand in Heaven, 21 far above all rule and jurisdiction and power and dominion and every name not only in This World, but also in the World to Come, 22 and all things subjected under His feet, and he gave headship over all things to the Messianic Beyt Din, 23 which is his body, the completeness of all reality with all things complete.

2 1 You had been dead in the sins and guilty actions, 2 in which you then walked then, according to the era of This World, according to the rulers of the powers of the air, the spirits currently working in the Sons of Rebellion, 3 among whom we also conducted ourselves — in the lusts of our flesh, doing the things desired by the flesh and the understandings *[thereof], and were Children of Punishment as were all the rest.*

4 But Elohim is abounding in mercy because of the greatness of His love with which he loved us 5 and, even though we were dead in our disobedience, He made us alive again by joining us with Messiah in His resurrection]. By chesed you are being saved, 6 and raised with Messiah and seated in Heaven with Messiah, in Messiah, Yshuà, 7 to demonstrate in the ages that are coming the exceeding abundance of His chesed, in goodness towards us in Messiah Yshuà, 8 because, by chesed you are saved through your moral conviction, but this is not from you, of Elohim is this gift, 9 not by labor, lest anyone brag. 10 For we are created by Him in Messiah Yshuà on the foundation of the Mitzvot, in which Elohim had already ordained for us to walk.

11 Therefore, remember you were Goyim in the flesh — those called "Uncircumcised" by those who are called "Circumcised" whose flesh was made so by hand, 12 that you were at that time without Messiah, having been alienated from the community of Israel, and strangers to the promise of the Covenant, hopeless and godless in the world.

13 But now, in Messiah, Yshuà, you, those who were far off, became near by the blood of Messiah, 14 for He himself is our peace — making both one, having broken the Middle Wall of partition. 15 Having destroyed in His flesh the opposition to the Torah, with its Commandments in Chukim, the two, He molds into one new people, making peace, 16 and reconciling both in one body to Elohim through the stake, killing the hostility in Himself.

17 Also, coming, He proclaimed "Peace, peace for the far
and for the near," 18 because through Him, we both have
access to the Father in one spirit.

19 Therefore, certainly, you are no longer strangers and
aliens, but fellow citizens of Elohim's People and of the House
of Elohim, 20 having built upon the foundation of the
representatives and the Prophets, the cornerstone being the
Messiah, Yshuà, Himself, 21 in whom, all the building is fitted
together, and grows into a Holy Temple in Adonai, 22 in
whom, you are being built together into the House of Elohim
in spirit!

3 1 Because of this, I, Shaul, prisoner of Messiah, Yshuà,
on behalf of you, the Gerim. 2 Surely, you have heard of the
chesed of Elohim, given to me, 3 so that by way of revelation
was made known to me the mystery as I wrote before in brief,
4 reading about which, you are able to understand my
knowledge of the mystery of Messiah, 5 which in other
generations was not made known to the sons of men as in the
manner that it has now been revealed to His representatives
and prophets in the Spirit: 6 the Gerim are co-heirs, and parts
of the same body, and co-participants of His promise in
Messiah through HaBsorat.

7 I became a messenger of this [HaBsorat] according to the
gift of Elohim's chesed, given to me according to the work of
His power. 8 To me, the least the Blessed Ones, was given this
chesed: to announce among the Gerim the unimaginable
vastness of the blessings of the Messiah, 9 and to bring to light
all that is the partnership of the mystery that was hidden
from the ages in Elohim, Who created all things, 10 that can
now be known to the principalities and authorities in Heaven,

through the Messianic Rabbinate, the diverse wisdom of
Elohim, 11 according to the purpose of the ages which He made
in Messiah, Yshuà, Adonaynu, 12 in whom, we have boldness
and access in confidence [to Elohim], through His moral
conviction. 13 Therefore, I ask you not to be weak as a result
of my troubles on your behalf which is your glory.

14 By reason of this, I bend my knees to the Father, 15 from
whom every family in Heaven and on Earth is named. 16 So
that He may give to you from the abundance of His glory to
become strength by the power of His Spirit within your inner
being, 17 so that the Messiah may dwell in your hearts through
your moral conviction, in love being rooted and settled, 18 so
that you, will be strengthened to comprehend, with all the
Sanctified Ones, the width, and the length, and the depth,
and the height, 19 to know the knowledge that goes beyond the
normal boundaries of knowledge of Messiah's love, so that you
may be filled to all the fullness of Elohim.

20 And to Him who is beyond able to do all things, to
accomplish more than we ask or imagine, 21 His is the glory in
the Messianic Rabbinate in the Messiah Yshuà to all
generations of the era of the eras. Amen.

4 *1 Therefore I, the prisoner in Adonai, implore walk in*
with all modesty and humility, with patience, upholding each
other in love, 3 being eager to preserve the unity of the Spirit
in the bond of peace. 4 One body and one Spirit, just as you
were called you were called in one hope of your calling, 5 one
Rebe, one moral conviction, one immersion, 6 and one Elohim,
the Father of all, El Shaddai. 7 To each one of us was given
chesed to the measure of the gift of Messiah. 8 Therefore it
says,

"You went up on high
You have led the exiles captive,
You took gifts of man."

[9] Now, "You went up," what is it unless He also went
down into the lower parts of the earth? [10] He coming down is
also He coming up up, far above all the heavens, so that He
could complete all things. [11] And He provided some
representatives, and some prophets, and some evangelists, and
some shepherds and rabbis [12] for the maturing of the
Sanctified People, for the work of ministry to build the body
of the Messiah, [13] until we all attain unity of moral conviction
and the knowledge of the Son of Elohim, to a man fully
formed to the measure of the stature of the completeness of
Messiah, [14] that we may no longer be small children being
blown about and carried away by every wind of doctrine, by
the schemes of man in trickery in the trap of error. [15] Instead,
telling the truth in love, we may grow in all things into Him
who is the head, Messiah, [16] by whom all of the body is being
fitted together and united through every bond supplied
according to the working in the measure of each part,
producing the growth of the body, building itself up in love.

[17] Therefore I say this and attest in Adonai: no longer
will you walk as the Gentiles walk, in the vanity of their
minds, [18] having been darkened in intellect, being alienated
from the life of Elohim, through the ignorance in them, which
results from the callous stupidity of their hearts, [19] who having
rejected joy, give themselves up to lust, to working all
uncleanness with greediness. [20] But you learned the complete
opposite of that: Messiah! [21] In fact, you heard Him and were
taught about Him, that the truth in Yshuà is: [22] cast off of you

*the former behavior of the old man, corrupted through lust
and delusion, 23 to be reformed in your spirits and your
minds, 24 and put on the new person, the one created
according to Elohim, in the righteousness and the holiness of
the truth.*

*25 Therefore, lay aside falsehood, each of you speak the
truth with his neighbor, because we are parts of the same
body. 26 Be angry, but don't sin; don't let the sun set on your
anger, 27 nor give an opportunity the Traducer.*

*28 Do not let the thief steal any longer; instead, command
him to labor well by hand, so that he will have something to
give those in need.*

*29 Do not allow any condemning, worthless words come
from your mouth, but only any good [words] to edify those in
need that may stir up chesed to those hearing. 30 And do not
grieve the Ruach Elohim HaKadosh, by whom you were
attested for a judgment of redemption. 31 Extinguish in you
all bitterness, and rage, and vengeance, and outcry, and
Lashon HaRa with all evil things. 32 And, be kind
sympathetic, and forgiving to each other yourselves, as
Elohim, in Messiah, forgave you.*

*5 1 Therefore be imitators of Elohim, as beloved children; 2
and walk in love, just as Messiah loved us, and surrendered
himself for us, as an offering, and a sacrifice to Elohim with a
pleasing aroma. 3 But as is fitting the Sanctified People, do
not allow sexual sins and all uncleanness and greediness to be
named among you, 4 and filthiness and speaking stupidly or
joking; but rather thanksgiving. 5 For know this: everyone
that is a sexual sinner, or unclean or a greedy person who is
an idol-worshiper, has inheritance in the Kingdom of the*

Messiah and Elohim. [6] Let no one deceive you with empty
words; for through these comes the punishment of Elohim
upon the Sons of Rebellion. [7] Therefore do not be their co-
participants.

[8] For you were then darkness; but now, light through
Adonai; walk as children of light. [9] For the fruit of the light
is in all goodness, righteousness and truth, [10] proving what is
fully agreeable to Adonai. [11] And do not share company with
the unfruitful works of darkness, but rather reprove [them], [12]
for it is shameful to even speak of the hidden things they do.
[13] But all things that are reproved are revealed by the light,
[14] This is why it says,

"Arise, sleeping one!
Stand up from the dead,
and Messiah will shine on you!"

[15] Therefore, watch carefully how you walk — not as the
unwise, but as the wise. [16] Improve the opportunity of the
time, because the age is evil. [17] Because of this, do not bestupid,
but understand what the will of Adonai is.

[18] And do not get drunk in wine in which there is complete
debauchery, but be filled with the Spirit — [19] speaking to
yourselves in Psalms, religious odes, and spiritual cantillation,
singing and playing music in your heart to Adonai; [20] always
give thanks for everything to God the Father in the name of
our Lord Yshuà the Messiah.

[21] Submit to each other in awe of the Messiah. [22] Wives
submit to your husbands as to Adonai, [23] because the man is
head of the wife, as also Messiah, is head of the [Messianic]
Rabbinate, and He is savior to the body. [24] But as the

*[Messianic] Rabbinate is submitted to Messiah, so also are the
wives to their husbands in everything.*

*25 The husbands, love the wives, just as the Messiah loved
the [Messianic] Community and surrendered Himself up on its
behalf, 26 so that he could sanctify it, cleansing the Mikveh, as
per the Oral Word, 27 that it could present to Him in glory the
[Messianic] Community having no defilement or wrinkle or
any such thing, but that it be holy and unblemished. 28 In
this way husbands are obligated: to love their wives as much
as they love their own bodies; he that loves his wife is loving
himself. 29 Because, no one ever hates his own flesh; he
nourishes it and cherishes it, just as the Messiah [does] the
[Messianic] Community, 30 because we are members of His
body. 31 "Therefore a man will leave his father and mother
and cling to his wife, and the two will become one flesh." 32
This is great mystery, but I speak concerning Messiah and the
[Messianic] Community, 33 but also, concerning you, each
and everyone: love his wife as himself, and wife revere the
husband.*

6 *1 Children, obey your parents, for this is right in
Adonai. 2 "Honor your father and mother" which is the first
Commandment with a promise 3 "that it may be well with
you, and that you may be long lived in the Land."*

*4 Fathers, do not provoke your children but make them,
but nurture them in education and the Torah of Adonai.*

*5 Slaves, obey your physical masters with fear, and
trembling in sincerity of your heart as to Messiah, 6 not after
the manner of sight-labor, as sycophants but as servants of
Messiah, doing Elohim's will from [your] soul, 7 serving with
kindness as to Adonai and not men, 8 knowing that*

whomsoever does this will get benefit from Adonai, whether slave of freeman.

9 And masters, treat your slaves the same way. Don't threaten them. Remember that in heaven both you and they have the same Master, and he has no favorites.

10 In conclusion, my brothers, be strengthened in Adonai, and in the power of His strength! 11 Put on the full armor of Elohim, to be able to stand against the trickery of the Traducer. 12 because we are not wrestling against flesh and blood, but against the principalities, and powers and against This World's rulers of darkness, against the spiritual evil in the high places. 13 Because of this, take up the full armor of Elohim; so that you will be able to resist in the day of evil, and stand, having accomplished absolutely all. 14 Therefore, stand, having girded your waist with truth, and putting stand, having girded your waist with truth, and putting on the put on breastplate of righteousness, 15 and having shod your feet with the preparation of the Bsorat of peace. 16 Above all having taken up the shield of moral conviction, by which you will be able to quench all the arrows that the Evil One ignites. 17 And take the helmet of Salvation, and the sword given by the Spirit, which is the Word of Elohim; 18 Through all, pray and petition, praying all the time, in the Spirit, and for the same thing guarding without fail and petitioning for all the Sanctified People, 19 and me, that I may be given speech when I open my mouth, in boldness to make known the mystery of the Bsorat, 20 for the sake of which, I am an ambassador in chains that in it I may speak boldly, in the manner that it is necessary for me to speak.

*[21] So that you may now, also know the things about me —
what I am doing, Tychicus, the beloved brother and a
trustworthy shamash in Adonai, will make all things known
to you. [22] Whom I sent to you, for this same thing, so that
you may know the things about us, and invoke comfort in
your heart.*

*[23] Peace to the brothers, and love with moral conviction in
Elohim Abba and Adonai Yshuà HaMashiach. [24] Chesed with
all those loving Adoneynu Yshuà HaMashiach in
immortality.*

Appendices

Appendix One:
Rabbi Hillel's Seven Rules of Interpretation

1: Kal VaChomer - argument from minor to major and vice versa.

The conditions that apply to a minor case of a principle or Mitzvah apply to an even greater degree to a major case of the same principle or Mitzvah.

2: Gezeirah shavah - argument by analogy.
(Equivalence of expressions)

An analogy is made between two separate texts on the basis of a similar phrase, word or root. Where the same words are applied to two separate cases, it follows that the same considerations apply to both.

3: Binyan av - Building up a "family"

A standard passage serving as a basis for interpretation of several commandments relating to the same matter. This is used so that we understand that no Commandment contradicts another. When we compare all commandments or passages concerning a particular topic all must be understood to agree with each other.

(4) Kelal ufrat - The general and the particular
This is the general and particular limitation of the general by the particular and vice versa.

When a general rule is given, and a specific condition is mentioned. The general rule is clarified by the specific condition.

(5) Sh'enei ketuvim – two writings

Two passages seem to contradict until nuances of either or a third passage show that they are actually in harmony. Rabbi Ishmael did not bother to includes the use of nuances since such nuances should have been fully investigated before the idea of a conflict came to mind.

(6) Ke yotzei bo mimakom acher - like that in another place –

The explanation of one passage according to another of similar word use. Since many words in Hebrew have multiple definitions, determining the intended meaning of a word in one passage may require consultation of the same wording from another passage on an unrelated topic.

(7) Davar halameid mi'inyano - definition from context."

The meaning of a passage may be deduced from its context within the same sentence or from another reference in the same passage.

Appendix Two:
Rabbi Ishmael's Thirteen Rules of Interpretation

1. Kal VaChomer (Light and heavy)

The Kal VaChomer rule says that what applies in a less important case will certainly apply in a more important case.

The Rabbinical writers recognize two forms of Kal VaChomer:

Kal VaChomer Meforash - In this form the Kal VaChomer argument appears explicitly. A Kal VaChomer Meforash argument is signaled by a phrase like "how much more..."

Kal VaChomer Satum - In which the Kal VaChomer argument is only implied. This lacks an obvious identifying phrase.

2. G'zerah Shavah (Equivalence of expressions)

An analogy is made between two separate texts on the basis of a similar phrase, word or root. Where the same words are applied to two separate cases, it follows that the same considerations apply to both.

3. Binyan ab mikathub echad (Building up a "family" from a single text)
Binyab ab mishene ketuvim (Building up a "family" from two or more texts)
A principle is found in several passages serving as a basis for interpretation of several commandments

relating to the same matter. This is used so that we understand that no Commandment contradicts another. When we compare all commandments or passages concerning a particular topic all must be understood to agree with each other. This differs from Binyab av mishene echad in that there is no single passage that explains the topic, but rather many passages all give elements that work together.

Binyan av mikathub echad (Building up a "family" from a single text)
A standard passage serving as a basis for interpretation of several commandments relating to the same matter. This is used so that we understand that no Commandment contradicts another. When we compare all commandments or passages concerning a particular topic all must be understood to agree with each other. This differs from Binyab av mishene ketuvim in that a single passage is the key to the entire topic.

4. Kelal uferat (The general and the particular)

   When a general rule is given, and a specific condition is mentioned. The general rule is clarified by the specific condition.

5. Perat ukhelal (particular and general).
   If the particular instances are stated first and are followed by the general category, instances other than the particular ones mentioned are included.

EXAMPLE:
Ex. 22:9 *"...an ass, or an ox, or a sheep, OR ANY BEAST"* beasts other than those specified are included.

Simply put: if a list is given and then the category is described, all things which fit into the category are included and the list is composed of examples of the types of things included in the general category. In the case above the list includes both kosher and treif animals.

6. Kelal uferat ukhelal i attah dan ella ke-ein ha-perat (general, particular, general)

   When the examples are bracketed by statement and restatement of the general rule, the listed examples are not just examples; that are part of the definition of the general rule.

7. Kelal she-hu tzarikh liferat uferat she-hu tzarikh li-khelal
   (The general requires the particular and the particular the general)
   Specification is provided by taking the general and the particular together, each requiring the other.

   Simply put: If the particular is a specification of the general rule that is a further explanation, both work together to define the general.

8. Davar she-hayah bi-khelal ve-yatza min ha-kelal lelammed lo lelammed al atzmo yatza ella lelammed al hakelal kullo yatzo

(If a particular instance of a general rule is singled out for special treatment, whatever is postulated of this instance is to be applied to all the instances embraced by the general rule.)

This means that both passages state the same Mitzvah and thus what applies to the particular applies to all other instances of the general rule.

9. Davar she-hayah bi khelal ve-yatza liton to'an echad she-hu khe-inyano yatza lehakel ve-lo lehachmir
(When particular instances of a general rule are treated specifically, in details similar to those included in the general rule, then only the relaxations of the general rule and not its restrictions are to be applied in those particular instances.)

Simply put: The similarity of language indicates that these are part of the same Mitzvah.

The particular may be an unusual case of the same Mitzvah where additional divine mercy applies, but we do not assume an increase of divine severity.

10. Davar she-hayah bi-khelal ve-yatza liton to'an acher she-lo khe-inyano yatza lehakel-lehachmir.
(When particular instances of a general rule are treated specifically in details dissimilar from those included in the general rule, then both relaxations and restrictions are to be applied in those particular instances)

Simply put: If the wording is dissimilar, each passage is a standalone Mitzvah even if the two are mechanically very similar.

11. Davar she-hayah bi-khelal ve-yatza lidon ba-davar he-chadash i attah yakhol lehachatziro li khelalo ad she-yachazirennu ha-katav li-khelalo be-ferush.
(When a particular instance of a general rule is singled out for completely fresh treatment, the details of the general rule must not be applied to this instance unless Scripture specifically says that it is to be applied.)

Simply put: A Completely fresh treatment does not need another passage to be understood because it is a separate Mitzvah.

12. Davar ha-lamed me-inyano ve-davar ha-lamed mi-sofo.
(The meaning of a passage may be deduced from (a) its context, or (b) from a later reference in the same passage)

This modification of Hillel's seventh rule: Davar hilmad me'anino (Explanation obtained from context) specifies that "context" can include adjacent verses on the same topic rather than just the same sentence. This can be assumed to be true in Hillel's wording we well.
The meaning of a passage may be deduced from its context within the same sentence or from another reference in the same passage.

The Scriptures are given as one continuous body of teaching from HaShem; they should be read as such.

13. Shenei khetuvim hamakhchishim zeh et teh ad she-yavo ha-katuv ha-shelishi ve-yakhria beineihem.

(Two verses contradict one another until a third verse reconciles them.)

Since truth cannot disagree with truth, no two verses of the Bible may contradict one another. If this appears to be the case there will always be a third verse that demonstrates that the two original passages actually agree with each other.

Appendix Three:

Rav Eliezer Ben Yose HaGalili's Thirty-Two Rules of Interpretation

(Taken from the public domain version of the "Jewish Encyclopedia")

Rules laid down by R. Eliezer b. Jose Ha-Gelili for haggadic exgesis, many of them being applied also to halakhic interpretation.

1. **Ribbuy** (extension): The particles "et", "gam", and "af", which are superfluous indicate that something which is not explicitly stated must be regarded as included in the passage under consideration, or that some teaching is implied thereby.

2. **Mi'ut** (limitation): The particles "ak", "rak", and "min", indicate that something implied by the concept under consideration must be excluded in a specific case.

3. **Ribbuy ahar ribbuy** (extension after extension): When one extension follows another it indicates that more must be regarded as implied.

4. **Mi'ut ahar mi'ut** (limitation after limitation): A double limitation indicates that more is to be omitted.

5. **Kal va-chomer meforash**: "Argumentum a minori ad majus", or vice versa, and expressly so characterized in the text.

6. **Kal va-chomer satum**: "Argumentum a minori ad majus" or vice versa, but only implied, not explicitly declared to be one in the text. This and the preceeding rule are contained in the Rules of Hillel number 1.

7. Gezerah shawah: Argument from analagy. Biblical passages containing synonyms or homonyms are subject, however much they differ in other respects, to identical definitions and applications.

8. Binyan ab mi-katub ehad: Application of a provision found in one passage only to passages which are related to the first in content but do not contain the provision in question.

9. Derek Kezarah: Abbreviation is sometimes used in the text when the subject of discussion is self-explanatory.

10. Dabar shehu shanuy (repeated expression): Repitition implies a special meaning.

11. Siddur she-nehlak: Where in the text a clause or sentence not logically divisible is divided by the punctuation, the proper order and the division of the verses must be restored according to the logical connection.

12. Anything introduced as a comparison to illustrate and explain something else itself receives in this way a better explanation and elucidation.

13. When the general is followed by the particular, the latter is specific to the former and merely defines it more exactly. (compare with Hillel #5)

14. Something important is compared with something unimportant to elucidate it and render it more readily intelligible.

15. When two Biblical passages contradict each other the contradiction in question must be solved by reference to a third passage.

16. Dabar meyuhad bi-mekomo: An expression which occurs in only one passage can be explained only by the context. This must have been the original meaning of the rule, although another explanation is given in the examples cited in the baraita.

17. A point which is not clearly explained in the main passage may be better elucidated in another passage.

18. A statement with regard to a part may imply the whole.

19. A statement concerning one thing may hold good with regard to another as well.

20. A statement concerning one thing may apply only to something else.

21. If one object is compared to two other objects the best part of both the latter forms the tertium quid of comparison.

22. A passage may be supplemented and explained by a parallel passage.

23. A passage serves to elucidate and supplement its parallel passage.

24. When the specific implied in the general is especially excepted from the general, it serves to emphasize some property characterizing the specific.

25. The specific implied in the general is frequently excepted from the general to elucidate some other specific property, and to develop some special teaching concerning it.

26. Mashal (parable).

27. Mi-ma'al: Interpretation through the preceding.

28. Mi-neged: Interpretation through the opposite.

29. Gematria: Interpretation according to the numerical value of the letters.

30. Notarikon: Interpretation by dividing a word into two or more parts.

31. Postposition of the precedent. Many phrases which follow must be regarded as properly preceding, and must be interpreted accordingly in exegesis.

32. May portions of the Bible refer to an earlier period than to the sections which precede them, and vice versa.

These thirty-two rules are united in the so-called Baraita of R. Eliezer b. Jose HaGelili. In the introduction to the Midrash ha-Gadol, where this baraita is given, it contains thirty-three rules. Rule 29 being divided into three, and rule 27 being omitted.

Appendix Four: The Forty-Two Rules of the Zohar

The Forty-Two Rules of the Zohar draw conclusions from poetic devices and from Gamatria, the study of the numerical value of the words in the original text.

I have chosen not to publish these rules because if a person has not yet studied the Tanakh, the Messianic Scriptures, the Talmud, and the Midrash attempting to use the Forty-two Rules of the Zohar could lead that person into serious misconceptions and theological error.

Additionally, the Messianic Scriptures were not preserved with the precise attention to detail demonstrated in the preservation of the Torah. This being the case, these rules cannot be applied to the Messianic Scriptures reliably.

Appendix Five:
The Four levels of Rabbinical Literature and Torah Interpretation

It has been noted that each of the four Bsorat (Gospels) is targeted to a different level of rabbinical interpretation. This is correct, but it should also be noted that all four levels of interpretation are applicable to each of the Bsorat.

Theses foul levels are:

Pashat (Simple)
This level of interpretation uses the simple grammar of the text. Hillel's Seven Rules are used for interpreting at this level.

This level of reading typically answers the question, "what do we have to do?"

Pashat interpretation establishes HaShem's Law.

The Bsorat Marcus (Mark) is best interpreted at this level.

Remez (Hint)
This level of interpretation is Allegoric. It draws meaning from extra letters, extra words, missing letters, missing words, larger letters, smaller letters, spacing between letters and words, letters written in an unusual way, dots or markings not explained by proper grammar. This utilizes the Thirteen Laws of Ishmael ben Eliezer.

Interpretation on this level typically answers the question, "What is the meaning behind what we have to do?"

Remez interpretation explains HaShem's Law.

The Bsorat Lucien (Luke) is best interpreted at this level.

Drash (Explore / Ask)
This level of interpretation uses a "parabolic logic" studying events and revelations in the Scripture to build up a base of knowledge to use when studying the Scriptures. This level of interpretation draws meaning from logical analysis of biblical events and the application of this analysis to words and phrases of the Scripture. This utilizes Rav Eliezer Ben Yose HaGalili's Thirty-Two Rules of Interpretation.

Interpretation on this level typically answers the questions, "How is HaShem's kingdom established on earth? How do we contribute to it? How do we actively become part of it?"

Drash interpretation leads us to spiritual improvement through HaShem's Law._

The Bsorat Mattityahu (Matthew) is best interpreted at this level.

Sod (Secret)
This level of interpretation takes a mystical approach to studying Scripture. The word "mystical" is not

meant in the occult sense here; rather, it is meant in the sense of investigating a mystery. Of course one must be fully grounded in the facts learned from more basic studies of the text before one can use this level of interpretation accurately. This level of interpretation draws meaning from a spiritual/metaphysical analysis of the scriptures based on poetic devices. This utilizes the Forty-Two Laws of the Zohar.

This level of reading typically answers the question, “What is the metaphysical meaning of what is happening as HaShem’s kingdom is established?”

Sod interpretation explains the mechanism of the spiritual improvement.

The Bsorat Yochanan (John) is best interpreted at this level.

Appendix Six:
Blasphemy Against the Holy Spirit

Since the Temple System requires different Offerings for "sins" and for "guilts," even though both actions are violations of God's Law, the difference must be important. In this passage Rabbi Shaul demonstrates that he feels the difference is important even after Yshu`a gave His life for our sins and guilts. In the biblical sense, "sins" are violations that occur because the person does not know the Commandment in question, and "guilts" are violations that occur when the person is trying to do the right thing, but is overcome with temptation. There is a third form of violation of God's Law which is discussed in Number 15:30-31.

"The soul who acts with a defiant hand, from out of the native, from out of the Ger, he blasphemed HaShem. That soul will be cut off from the midst of the People. Because the word of HaShem he has disesteemed and broken a Miztvah, utterly cut off and cut off that soul will be; His sin will be upon him."

First the good news: This is not any intentional violation of Torah; it is an arrogant and defiant violation. This means that it is unrepentant. The Torah (Exodus 34:6 & 34:7) HaShem forgives even willful, and cleanses but not completely. Based on the Teachings of Yshu`a, we would conclude that repentance is the dividing point between cleansing and lack of cleansing. We see this in the requirements of the Guilt Offering. Since the Torah gives no time limit on this, we can justifiably assert that as long as remorse comes before death, that forgiveness is still possible.

Now the scary news: The phrase "*that soul will be cut off*" refers to damnation. What is more, in biblical Hebrew doubling a word intensifies its meaning. In verse 31, "karet (cut off)" is doubled with the second usage being a more intense form.

This is followed by the phrase "his sin will be upon him" which obviously indicates that this sin remains upon the soul even in the next life. According to Sifre, this means that the sin taints the soul and keeps it out of the World to Come. Rashi agreed with this, but added that repentance would wipe the sin away and prevent the punishment from being executed.

It is also important to note that the definite article "ha" is not used in the Hebrew in conjunction with the word "Mitzvah." There is no other word in the verse that would indicate a specific Mitzvah as the specific action being taken by the blasphemer. Therefore this defiant spirit can be manifest in the violation of any of the Mitzvot, as long as the defiant spirit is motivation the action.

I used "disesteemed" in translation because it is a single word that fairly captures the meaning of the Hebrew word "bazah" which means "to hold in less regard that deserved" or "to despise" or "to scorn." The definition is chosen by context. Since the action may hold no particular hatred of ridicule for the Word of HaShem, all that remains is simply not giving the Word of the All-Mighty the respect He and His Word deserves.

We also know that in Matthew 12:31&32, Yshu`a said that all violations are forgivable except "blasphemy against the

Holy Spirit." At first one might think that Matthew 12:31&32 contradicts Numbers 15:30&31, even though we know that truth cannot contradict truth.

This apparent contradiction is resolved using Rabbi Ishmael ben Eliezer's Thirteenth Rule of Interpretation, "*Two verses contradict one another until a third verse reconciles them.*" This rule is a clarification of Rabbi Hillel's Seventh Rule of Interpretation, "*Analogy made from another passage.*" The third passage that we find discusses unforgivable sin using the definition found in Numbers 15:30&31 and the nomenclature found in Matthew 12:31&32.

Hebrews 10:26-29 "*And let us do this all the more as you see the Day approaching. For if we deliberately continue to sin after receiving the knowledge of the truth, there no longer remains a sacrifice for sins, but only the terrifying prospect of Judgment, of raging fire that will consume the enemies. Someone who disregards the Torah of Mosheh (Moses) is put to death without mercy on the word of two or three witnesses. Think how much worse will be the punishment deserved by someone who has trampled underfoot the Son of G-d; who has treated as something common the blood of the Covenant which made him holy; and who has blasphemed against the Holy Spirit, giver of G-d's grace!*"

Since we know that The Father, the Messiah and the Holy Spirit are one, we can understand how these terms can mean the same thing, and the passage in Hebrews brings them together and proves that these passages actually agree.

Now that we understand that in the Gospels and in the Torah the same action is referred to as unforgivable, we must know what this action is. The subtleties of the original Hebrew text of Numbers 15:30&31 indicate that this violation is committed with knowledge of the quality of one's actions and with knowledge of God, with an attitude of arrogance and defiance, and with a complete lack of regret. This agrees with the author of Hebrews, who tells us that only those who are first saved can loose salvation permanently.

On the optimistic side, the Torah does not set a time limit on this feeling of regret. The description of the Guilt Offering is Leviticus gives us the difference between a guilt and this blatant defiance. The violator must repent before he is caught and brought to judgment. Our final judgment comes after we die. Therefore, anyone who genuinely regrets committing any evil action can be forgiven; only those who refuse to admit that it is God who defines what is good and what is evil are lost, and even these may repent of their error as long as they live.

Appendix Seven: Gentiles are not Goyim

The term Goyim has been used to refer to Gentiles, however this application is not biblically accurate. On the flip side of this coin is the fact that many Christians claim to be "grafted into Israel" when in fact they are not. As is typical when humans invent extremes, the truth is in the middle.

To discover the truth, it is best to go to the source of truth, the Bible. The Bible refers to several groups of people in the broader spiritual sense. These are Yhudim, Gerim, Toshavim, Goyim, and those who are Karet (cut off). Based on our english wording, Gerim, Toshavim, and Goyim, are all Gentiles. So, while SOME Gentiles are Goyim, others are not.

To further understand this and to understand the place of Gentiles within the Messianic movement and within the body of Messiah, we need to understand each of these words found in the Torah. This is particularly important because a Messianic Jew who correctly understands the Biblical status of Gentiles will tend to be more accepting of those Gentiles who seek to truly graft into Israel – not just with words or slogans but with actual actions and theological conviction. Additionally, a Gentile who is aware of his position and aware of the correct, biblical definitions of the three words used for different types of Gentiles may be inspired to come closer to God and become truly grafted in.

Let us begin or discussion of all five groups of people in this biblical list…

Yhudim are religious Jews. The Yehudim and Jews who are physically descended from Avraham, Yitzchak and Ya`akov, and who maintain the Covenant. The modern term "religious Jews" opens the possibility for the existance of "non-religious Jews." The Bible does not open such a possibility. This is stated over and over in the Torah as well as in Rabbi Shaul's writings. If a Jew rejects Judaism, he is Karet (cut off from his people). A former Jew who is Karet is spiritually lower than the lowest Gentile idolater. It is possible that the Gentile idolater has never been told about HaShem, but the person who is karet knew better.

Now we go on to the three categories of Gentiles…

The word "Goyim" is the most familiar to most people. Literally, "Goyim" simply means "nations." However, after the formation of Israel, the word took on a meaning that implies paganism. Specifically, there was one nation that worshiped HaShem, and that was Israel. The plural use of the word was used for pagan nations. When referring to an individual, Goy always means "a person of the pagan nations." In short, "Goyim" are idolaters.

While it can honestly be said that Gentiles who worship idols or even an Atheist are Goyim, not all Gentiles do so.

Now we got to less universally familiar biblical words. We begin with "Toshavim" or "Toshav" for the singular. Toshavim are people who have rejected idolatry and acknowledge HaShem as God, but who have not accepted the Covenant. Toshavim were allowed to live and work in Israel. However, in Leviticus Chapter Twenty-Two, the Torah says that they were treated as unclean with respect to the Holy things of the Temple. In Exodus, Chapter Twelve,

Toshavim are forbidden to partake of the Passover Offering.

Today's Toshavim would be those Christians who reject idolatry, but who do not fell compelled to accept the Covenant and the responsibilities that go along with accepting the Covenant.

Finally we get to the Gerim. Gerim are people of Gentile descent who reject idolatry, accept HaShem as the one true God, and who choose to enter into the Covenant. The Torah says many times over "There is one Law for the Native born and for the Ger." Gerim are not only allowed to participate in the Passover they are required to do so. Gerim are grafted into Israel, or as Rabbi Shaul puts it in Romans "grafted into the olive tree."

Obviously not all Gentile followers of Messiah are Gerim. Many believe that they are grafted into Israel simply by believing that Yshu`a is the Messiah, but the Bible makes it very clear that this is not the case. To truly be grafted into Israel, a Gentile must commit himself or herself to upholding all of the Commandments. This does not mean that the person has to be perfect. There are very few perfect people. It means that they have to be committed to following God.

The exact requirements of what changes a person from a Toshav to a Ger were not specifically given in the Torah, but some requirements were. So, the Sages attempted to fill in the gaps with extrapolation from scripture and considerable caution to help prevent people from going astray. This eventually resulted in the formal conversion process that exists within Orthodox Judaism today. It should be noted for non-Jewish readers that the Beyt Din that presides over the conversion does not have the authority to "make a conversion." The Beyt Din tests to see if HaShem has done a conversion. In the Messianic Scriptures we are are given additional information. We discover that the biblical process is based not on memorizing a list of prayers and Mitzvot; it is based on committing one's self to obeying God. This makes perfect sense if one has read the Torah. Israel accepted and pledged to obey all of His Commandments before God told the Children of Israel what those Commandments were. It only makes sense that the individual experience of a Gentile becoming grafted into Israel should parallel the experience of the Nation of Israel as God formed us.

Glossary

The Divine:

Adonai = Literally "Lord." G-d. This is used when the four letter name comes up in Torah reading or prayer.

Elohim = G-d. Literally "gods." Used in the Bible when G-d is acting in strict judgment. The plurality of this Hebrew word indicates the Unity of HaShem.

El Shadai = G-d. Literally "the All-Significant One (All-Powerful, All-Important, All-Knowing, Omnipresent)." This name is used when HaShem is doing miracles; it connotes His ability to override the physical laws.

HaShem = G-d. Literally, "HaShem" means "the Name." This is used instead of the four-letter name of G-d. Since we do not know the exact pronunciation of the four-letter name, we use "HaShem" as a sign of respect. Since we do not know the vowels, many Jews "dash out" the vowels in the more popular English euphemisms "G-d" and "L-rd."

Ruach HaKodesh = The Holy Spirit

Shkinah = the visible presence of G-d.

**Yshu\`a** = the Messiah. Also: "Rebbe Yshu\`a Ben Yosef" and "Yshu\`a HaMashiach" This name can also be transliterated "Yshua" or "Yeshua." The name "Yshu\`a" means "salvation." This is not the same as Yhoshu\`a, Yahoshu\`a, Yahashu\`a or any other variant that adds a ה ("H") sound. The addition of the ה changes the meaning to

"God is my salvation." Aside from not being historically accurate, this altered meaning does not make sense because Messiah is OUR salvation and he did not need saving.

The Word of G-d:

Tanakh = The scriptures that Christians refer to as "the Old Testament." When printed as a Tanakh, the order of the books is preserved. This order is based upon the level of divine inspiration. The Tanakh takes its name from the three sections of scripture that it contains: Torah, Nvi'im, Ketuvim.

Torah = The Instruction. The five books dictated to Mosheh by HaShem.

Nvi'im = The Prophets. In these books, HaShem made his word known to the prophets in dreams and visions. The prophets then explained the vision in their own words.

Ketuvim = The Holy Writings. The authors of these books were inspired in their hearts by HaShem. Some of these books contain some prophecies.

B'sorat = Good news (Gospel). This term can apply to either the Four Gospels specifically, or to the entire Ketuvim Meshiachim.

Ketuvim Meshiachim = The Messianic Scriptures. Christians refer to this as the "New Testament," but the teaching of Messiah is so grounded in Torah that it is not actually "New." Messiah explained things from the Torah that men had lost sight of or had failed to understand.

Talmud = The Talmud contains the Mishna, the Oral Torah, and the Gemmara, the discussion. There are two Talmuds: the Jerusalem Talmud and the Babylonian Talmud. The Mishna is the same in both, but the Gemmara is different. The Babylonian Talmud is about three times as large as the Jerusalem Talmud. Of these two, the Babylonian Talmud is considered more authoritative.

Mishna = The Oral Torah was first given to Mosheh who taught it to Aharon and Yohoshua ben Nun (Joshua). For centuries it was transmitted orally. After the Second Temple was destroyed the Mishna was compiled to ensure that the Oral Torah was not corrupted while the Jews were in exile. Despite the good intentions of the compilers, there is internal evidence that the oral transmission had already allowed errors to creep in. These errors are found in places where Beyt Hillel and Beyt Shammai disagree as to the correct Mishna on a topic and may be elsewhere as well.

Gemmara = The discussion that was added to the Mishna by the Ammorim to clarify the Mishna. The Gemmara is more than just a commentary on the Mishna. The Gemmara contains discussions on almost every aspect of life. To comment on this wide range of topics the Gemmara contains records of historical events, religious and ethical material, legends handed down in Jewish oral history, science, prayers and other materials. There are two versions of the Gemmara: the Babylonian and the Jerusalem. It is the Gemmara that differentiates between Talmud Bavli (Babylonian Talmud) and Talmud Yerushalami (Jerusalem Talmud).

Midrash = A combination of Jewish history and allegory that is used to help understand the Torah and the Tanakh. While technically, not given by HaShem, it does contain accounts of His actions and explanations the events in the Tanakh.

People:

Aharon = Aaron, the first Kohen Gadol (High Priest).

Gerim = converts to Judaism. These people fully accept the Covenant that God made with Avraham and became grafted into Israel. “Ger” is the masculine singular, and Gerah is the feminine singular.

Mosheh = Moses. The Prophet that G-d sent to lead the Jewish people out of Egypt

Rabbi Kefa = Peter. Trained and ordained by Yshu`a, Rabbi Kefa desired to maintain the purity of Messianic Judaism. Talmid of Yshu`a.

Rabbi Shaul = Paul. Trained at the feet of Rabban Gamliel the Elder, he was extremely well educated in Judaism. He had an educational level that today would be equivalent to Doctorates in Rabbinical Studies and Rabbinical Literature. Though not a Talmid of Yshua, Rabbi Sha`ul wrote many of the letters found in the Ketuvim Meshiachim.

**Rabbi Ya`akov ben Yosef** = James. Younger brother of Yshu`a and apparently leader of the Messianic Beyt Din (at least in Acts 15). Leader of a Messianic synagogue in Israel, and author of "The Letter of Ya`akov ben Yosef" ("James").

Rabbi Yochanan = John. Author of John, the First Letter of John, the Second Letter of John, the Third Letter of

John, and (most likely) Revelation. Talmid of Yshu`a. One of the three most respected leaders of Messianic Judaism in the First Century CE.

Talmidim = the Twelve Students or "Disciples" of Yshu`a. Singular: "Talmid"

Toshavim = “residents” - people of non-Jewish lineage who accept HaShem as God, but who have not chosen to enter into the Covenant.

Yochanan HaMatbil = (aka: "Yochanan the Immerser" and "John the Baptist") The son of Z'kharyah, the priest, who heralded the coming of Yshu`a.

Yhudah Ish Kiriot = (aka "Judas Escariot") An Edomite who was one of the twelve Talmidim for a while, but then betrayed Yshu`a to the Saducees who in turn gave Him to the Romans for trial and execution.

The Infernal:

Armillus = The Anti-Christ. The name "Armillus" is from the Aramaic for "Romulus," the founder of the Roman Empire and an Edomite. According to traditional Jewish interpretation of the Prophecies of Messiah, Messiah ben Yosef [who we know to be Yshu`a] would be killed by Armillus. Since Yshu`a was betrayed by an Edomite who accepted payment, convicted in a Roman (Edomite) Court under Roman (Edomite) Law, and executed by Roman (Edomite) Soldiers, this name has a certain significance. Also transliterated as: "Armilus."

B'liya`al = Satan. Literally this name means "Lawless/Rebellious/Worthless." This name stresses the character of Satan - his personality.

Geyhinnom = The place where the damned are confined after the Day of Judgment

HaMashchit = Satan. Literally "The Destroyer." This term acknowledges that Satan causes only destruction.

HaSatan = Satan. Literally, the word means "the Enemy [of G-d and Mankind]." This name indicates the political position of Satan as the Enemy of G-d and the Enemy of Mankind.

Sh`ol = Also "Sheol." The underworld or more accurately a place where the dead awaited judgment prior to the coming of Messiah. According to rabbinical writings, this place was divided into two compartments, one for those who would be damned and one for those who would be saved. (note: not all Rabbinical sources agree with each other)

Takhti = The area of Sh`ol reserved for those who would be damned on the Day of Judgment

Times:

Chanukkah = The Feast of Dedication. Ironically, this feast was rejected by Christianity and kept by Judaism despite the fact that the only biblical mention of the feast is in the book of Yochanan (John), when Messiah celebrated the feast.

Holy Days = The words "Holy Days" are used rather than the word "holidays" because we want to maintain our focus on the holiness of the days that G-d commanded us to celebrate.

Pesach = Passover (the entire week). This word is also used for the lamb offered to God on the Holy Day. The context of the sentence tells the reader which meaning to understand as one reads.

Rosh HaShannah = Head of the Year, Jewish New Year. Also called "Yom Teruah" (Day of Sounding [Shofars]) and "Feast of Trumpets"

Shabbat = Sabbath. Weekly, from sunset Friday to sunset Saturday.

Shavuot = Pentecost. The anniversary of the giving of the Ten Utterances (Ten Commandments). Later, the Holy Spirit was poured out on this day.

Simchat Torah = The Joy of the Torah. This Holy Day celebrates the the end of one cycle of Torah reading, and the beginning of another.

Sukkot = Feast of Tabernacles, also the time of the Birth of Messiah.

Yom HaBikkurim = Day of First Fruits, There were actually two of these one on Sukkot and one on the first work-day after the Passover Seder when the counting of the Omer begins. The Passover Yom HaBikkurim was also known as “Yom Reyshit” or “Reyshit HaOmer” and was the day of Messiah's Resurrection.

Yom Kippur = Day of Atonement. This specifically refers to national atonement.

Items:

Ammud = podium where the rabbi speaks

Aron = The Ark containing the Torah Scroll.

Bimah = .table for reading the Torah scroll during services.

Sefer Torah = Torah Scroll. An exact reproduction of the first Torah Scroll penned by Mosheh. Each letter is the same size, the same shape, and in the same position as the first Torah Scroll. This ensures that there are no errors.

Kippah = The Skull cap worn by Jewish men. This is worn in obedience to G-d's command that we shall not serve Him with our heads uncovered and with the knowledge that we are to serve Him at all times. Also called a "yarmulke."

Tallit (Tallis) = The four cornered garment upon which we affix Tzitzit. The word "Tallit" does not translate to English, but sometimes the nickname "Prayer shawl" is used as an "English-friendly" euphemism.

Tfillin = Small leather boxes containing scriptures passages written on small scrolls. These are worn during morning services except on Shabbat. Some people use a Greek word to refer to Tfillin, but the word does not mean Tfillin. Because that Greek word means "magic charm," it is improper and I will not even write it in this book.

Tzitzit = the “tassels” or “fringes” that God commands Jewish men to wear as a reminder of our responsibility to obey God.
This commandment is found in Number 15:37-41

Other:

Chesed = The Hebrew word "chesed" does not translate to English or Greek. The Greek word "kharis" was used to translate this word when the Brit Chadashah was translated into Greek. The Greek word "kharis" translates to the English word "graciousness (as "gratifying")." The Original Hebrew word, "chesed," means "acts of kindness motivated only by love." Since the Hebrew word expresses the concept so completely and exactly, many Messianic Believers prefer it to English words commonly used.

Kavanah = Intention. The reason or goal of a person's actions. The primary message of Yshu`a's earthly ministry was that there are only two valid kavanot for obeying any Mitzvah:

1. Love for HaShem
2. Love for one's fellow man

Kashrut = The laws of acceptability of foods. These laws were complied from biblical and extra-biblical sources. There are variations of opinion on some matters.

Mitzvah / Mitzvot = Commandment / Commandments. The 613 Commandments found in the Bible.

www.ingramcontent.com/pod-product-compliance
Ingram Content Group UK Ltd.
Pitfield, Milton Keynes, MK11 3LW, UK
UKHW041943190726
13854UKWH00004B/1766

9 781411 686021